AMONG THE PC

GARY ALAN MOTLEY

GW01402740

EXORDIUM

The following is the beginning of a beautiful love story in thirteen chapters. Each of those chapters is a short story and has a Latin heading relating to the text that follows.

Neither English nor Polish seemed to hold sway without cultural bias, so enigmatically, and since the whole is in itself a journey into the unknown, I chose Latin to emphasise this, being as it is here, a linguistic neutrality and that which can never really obtain linguistic equilibrium.

For Nan and Granddad who were love encapsulated. These words are yours.

I hope this will be the sort of English up with which the Polish will also put.

For someone who was always indifferent to foreign lands and their inhabitants, to end up living abroad seemed to be a somewhat hypocritical anachronism.

I had grown up in Kent and spent the first six years of my life happily wandering around the streets of Bexleyheath and Barnehurst, or as was more likely, being pushed around said streets by my mother and father. I have little memory of it but was told I attended a school near Bexleyheath called Normandy. A foreign-sounding name if ever I heard one. I remember that you had to climb this steep hill in order to get to this place of education, which must've been terrible for my poor old mum, carting me up there every day with my pushchair in tow. The houses around Bexleyheath all looked

1

quite similar. Stone-blasted, four windows and a lovely driveway. I liked Normandy and made a few good friends during my limited time there including my first ever girlfriend at the age of five. Rachael Williams. Long blonde hair and a beautiful smile. We walked up that blasted hill together every morning which perhaps wasn't as romantic as it sounded as she lived five doors up from us and was a good friend of the family. I also remember a giant playground just behind our house. With infrastructure that would simply not pass any safety regulations these days. A slide as high as a small house and an umbrella ride. Both outlawed as dangerous today. I didn't know danger at that age though. I spun around on that umbrella ride and slid down that slide onto the hard concrete ground below. I was sans fear. Bexleyheath also had a large park close to where my Nan and Granddad lived where we all used to play as kids. It has an immense boating lake where people can row boats and have races while pretending to be Oxford or Cambridge in the University Boat Race. I have always supported Oxford but am a little coy at admitting it these days as their reserve boat is rather unfortunately called ISIS. I don't wish to be seen as offering up sympathy for the Devil and all that bananas.

Presently around the middle of 1979 we decided to move down south. I left Bexleyheath, Barnehurst and Normandy behind me in what perhaps in later life would have been a hail of tears. For I liked those quintessential English environs. They felt 'right', through my six-year-old eyes. I suppose as I look back these places were more 'foreign' than I realised. Certainly living a marathon distance only away from the most multi-cultural place on planet Earth, (London - for those not yet familiar with Bexleyheath or Barnehurst) in comparison to the place we moved to that summer, I may as well have been living in Narnia. (Though C S Lewis1 never mentioned the Regal Cinema, the Clocktower or Danson Park).

We set up home, my mother, father, and little sister in the sleepy town of Fareham in the county of Hampshire. Back then I recall thinking in abject horror that we had moved into 'the heart of the forest.' I half expected to meet the Brothers Grimm2 on my way to school. I don't want to be overly critical about my adopted town but I imagine over the years it has probably rendered a few brothers grim. My father, Graham, a hard-working man in his early forties had found a job near Portsmouth and had decided to lead the way to the south coast along with Barbara, my mum, Carol my younger sister and a dog named Pip.

Fareham was and still is a small town on the south coast of England. Situated as it is between two sizeable commercial monoliths, Portsmouth and Southampton. In many ways picturesque. But in no way anything but indigenous. It seemed to me that everyone who lived in the town came from its belly. Was born, bred, nurtured and watered amongst its homely winding streets, deserted little alleys and quaint traditional country pubs.

In the early eighties came an addition to our family. A healthy baby boy whom my parents decided to christen Keith, possibly after Harris but equally plausible I suppose, after Moon or Richards. He became my brother of course and our lunacy and antics over the next two decades deserve another book in themselves.

I didn't ever dislike living in Fareham and made many friends therein, but I never really got over that 'lost in the forest' analogy encountered on my first few days there.

I noted above that my brother was a healthy boy although for the purposes of this narrative I must recall an enlightening tale. He did, as a small boy suffer from what must have been intolerable constipation, and as a result visited the doctor and sometimes even the hospital on various occasions. I feel personally that my life in Fareham has on reflection been a bit like suffering from this unfortunate affliction. I always knew that I wanted to get something out and I knew that there was no obvious obstruction to my achieving anything, but somehow Fareham would always hold me back just a little. The reader may of course allow himself a little chuckle at my outspoken remarks here but I stand firm. The analogy was and always has been there for me. So perhaps now that I'm actually putting pen to paper in this way and giving the world, or at least some of the twenty-seven or so nations of Europe, the chance to read over my literary outpourings, I have in some way taken a small dose of laxative.

I rattled through my school, teenage and early work years in a hail of misguided passion for life. I expect I did everything you would imagine a youth might do who had a zest for consuming energy, and an agreeable appearance. The tales of loves lost are a plenty, though once more the topic of another opus, I'm sure. To be honest such tales, I believe, are odious and tiresome and may only gauge the interest of an E L James3 fanatic. And since at no time did I ever engage in anything that saucy inker might have written about, no work of mine could ever do justice on that score.

Eschewing all the usual shenanigans anybody may envisage, up until mid-2004 I don't believe I ever had a vision, or a direction in life. I felt at one with a God or fate. He or it would decide my future and to hell with everything else. So it shall be written, so it shall be done. To an extent I still believe that.

But I now have a direction in life. I know now where I want to go and what I want to be.

When in 2004 the UK opened up its borders to Eastern Europe and of course a few of those Eastern Europeans came for 'want of a better life with residuals' and the promise of more stable weather, my life changed forever.

I met, in 2004, a beautiful young lady. She was in all respects the girl of my dreams. She was close to an ideal I had about women. She was attractive, dark, and clever (I'm in no way saying I didn't like the exact opposites. I have dated ugly, blonde dumb girls) and she liked heavy metal music. This was a girl I could identify with, for I too had always been partial to the wail of the electric guitar, the pound of the tom-tom drum, and the scream of the frontman charging around on stage all sweaty and aggressive. I liked that. It was different. It was me.

I subsequently moved to her country which happened to be Poland. But what you may be wondering was my inclination, what my motivation. How did I make the decision to leave all for a future I could hardly have imagined? How did I survive in the rugged country-land of Poland? How did I learn the language? What did I eat? How if it did, did it change my life? The short answer was simply that I fell in love. The longer answer, if you wish to persevere and have the time, is this....

CHAPTER ONE

NON SUM QUALIS ERAM

I was working hard one day. Working as I often did, minding my own business and probably whistling gaily to myself, as I checked off ready rooms on the computer and put vacant rooms back into the system. All ready for the men with fat wallets to come and desecrate the sheets and bedclothes with their blatant primal urges and their wilful blue-collar abandon. I was a hotel worker as you may have guessed. I worked shifts in several departments and by all accounts it was woeful. I don't mean the people. The folk who worked with me were nice. They were of a sunnier disposition than perhaps should have been the case when dealing with men with blatant primal urges and wilful blue-collar abandon.

It was a warm day in July 2004 when I thought I might take a spot of lunch, having just acquired a window through which to peer at the option of a hot meal and a sit-down.

I shuffled up to the staff canteen. I opened the door and inquisitively spied the day's dietary offerings brought in by the slightly dirty-looking kitchen porter with the scum-encrusted chef whites who frequently looked unkempt, unshaven and uninterested. I lost a lot of weight at that hotel.

I sat down at a table with what I thought might have been a safer bet. A sandwich with salad that appeared to have been covered over with cling film. Did the kitchen porter do it? What the heck. No one had yet died from the food laid out for staff, (that said I didn't really want to be the first).

I ate tentatively, glancing from time to time at the kitchen porter with suspicion dancing a jig across my boat race. A few other staff members drifted in and surveyed the food with differing degrees of frightful inquisition. A manager swaggered in, intelligently opened up a packed lunch and grinned at me knowingly as I munched upon my cheese and pickle butty with a coleslaw side. Then in came four young ladies I had not seen before. I looked in wonder. They seemed to be a bit lost and slightly unsure of themselves (not uncommon in that staff room as a rule). They sat down together and began to eat and amazingly, although only two yards away from them, I found to my horror I was incapable of overhearing anything from their conversation.

I thought little more of this at the time but over the following days I would meet the same four females again and again. In the lunch room. In the restaurant. In the corridors. I suppose I found out after a few days that they were not English. They were of a foreign clime. Once armed with this knowledge my interest was aroused. (To any Polish readers that last sentence was indeed intended as a cheeky Sid James-type play on words – English readers can take it as homework).

I learnt that two of these girls were from Slovakia and that the other two were sisters and from Poland. I noted that one of the girls from Slovakia was very tall and strangely that one of the Polish girls was also over 6 feet. I immediately erased these two, despite the fact that they were acceptably attractive, from my calculations. I don't like tall women that much. They unnerve me. So, left with the other two I set to work. Wooing them, as I did. Coincidently, these two shared the same name. Marta. Over the course of several days I coaxed Slovakian Marta out on a date. She was a shy 26 year old, about 5 foot 6 with dark hair and had come to the UK to work and improve her English, which I secretly thought was a good idea as at the time it wasn't that great. We went for a pizza which I imagined everyone could understand no matter where they came from. We sat in a lovely waterside bar, a bit pricey but no more than I thought I could afford, and over a pepperoni meat feast and a coffee conversed as best we could. When faced with a scenario like this you quickly learn that it's not

4

what you say but the manner in which you say it. Everything becomes dilated and simple. Your mind works on overdrive and sends out drivel you may have uttered as a five year old. And surprisingly Slovakian Marta appeared to appreciate my childish linguistic efforts. Either that or she just liked the pepperoni meat feast. It did have a deep crust. This revelation that I could hold my own when presented with a conversational barrier would later hold me in good stead when I came to be a teacher in Poland.

I was a bit worried in that restaurant though. I thought that Marta might see me as something I wasn't. A fool. Which perhaps I had been in the years leading up to this epiphany, when time suddenly skewed off on a tangent and from which it has still not turned back. Like in Back to the Future 2 when Doc explains how Biff used the Sports Almanac to alter the future and create an alternative 1985. I am living my alternative future right now and it started when I met these people.

Halfway through our little soiree I realised that I had to spend a penny. Unfortunately not on the pizza bill. That came to more than a few pennies I can tell you. I needed to used the wash room as it was probably called in this establishment. In this place the toilets were located upstairs and once inside you could as a man, (I never ventured into the ladies so can't vouch for what they may have experienced) stand and urinate whilst overlooking the restaurant and its clientele in all their finery down below, peering through what looked like a glass port hole such as you might have found on-board the Titanic. As I did so, I located Marta obliviously eating the pizza in the middle of the restaurant. She was still there. And remained there for the duration of my rather long-winded urination. She did not leave. I felt vindicated. I was doing alright. I knew no Slovakian, she very little English, but she wanted more of me. (I sincerely hope it wasn't that she was just a little broke and I had said that I would pay).

Following this date we met up again a few more times and spent a little time together. She soon left the hotel though and sadly we sort of drifted apart. This was mainly due to my wooing of Polish Marta, the second of the Martas. I kept my options open I believe back then, not really knowing what to expect from these girls and because of all the unnerving tall ones.

Polish Marta was 28. A little shorter at around 5 foot 4 with long dark hair. And attractive. There was no doubt about that. Similar I thought. In for a penny. She spoke English pretty well. Her language skills were rather good and we were able to have a conversation somewhat easier than the one I had had in the pizza restaurant. And I didn't need a glass port hole to check she was still interested from afar. She made a lot of the running! She was a brazen little minx. And I fell for her charms, foreign though they might have been. I romanced that girl from the off. We spent a lot of time together at work and out of work. We became over the next few weeks, quite the topic of conversation at the hotel. In no time at all by way of an energy I never knew I had, I learnt the Polish for 'hot, cold, hello, goodbye, thank-you, rock star, river, frog, cool, another pint please, (possible fuck-offs – she wouldn't say) etc. It was great fun. My days were suddenly bright again, I looked forward to going to work, and at last I could eat a cheese and pickle sandwich from the lunch room without fear, for I had met the Pole and life was about to take me on an express train on a yellow-bricked track to an Emerald city of adventure. Whether I would meet L Frank Baum4, I knew not, nor did I know there was to be no return to Kansas.

CHAPTER TWO

ARS GRATIA ARTIS

The late summer and onset of autumn 2004 was a heady time for me. I didn't really see it for what it was at the time but I undoubtedly fell in love. Polish Marta was as I have said, close to my ideal woman. We exchanged opinions and started to get to know each other a little better. The Polish sisters lent me some music to listen to whilst I whiled away the hours in my free time. They loved a band called Closterkeller and another one called Acid Drinkers, a Polish group that apparently sang and still sing in English. Over the coming months and years I got to experience these two groups first-hand and in many cases got to speak to the band members in and out of the Green Room.

After a couple of weeks the sisters asked me if I wanted to stay the night one Friday. They both lived in staff accommodation offered by the hotel we all worked for. The hotel had three of these places next to each other just across the road. I lived in one room in the middle house whilst Marta and her sister occupied a room in the adjoining abode. So in effect when asked whether or not I wanted to sleep over it wasn't as breathtakingly exciting as it could have been. I just nipped over the fence and they put the kettle on.

By mid-September things with the siblings and in particular Marta were going really well. I had slept over two or three times by this time and they had cooked for me on several occasions. Polish food on first experiencing it was rather interesting, appearing at first very basic but on closer inspection a cuisine all on its own. Vegetables, fish, breadcrumbs, meat, all thrown together in some cases. Of course I returned the favour and invited them over to my place where I cooked a lovely mixed salad (cooking a mixed salad is something to be proud of Jamie Oliver) fish soup, a stir fry and beef steak. This was followed by a couple of bottles of cheap Lambrini. (Is there an expensive kind?) We then proceeded to launch three sheets to the wind.

They were very impressed with my culinary efforts. The following morning I also learnt that one or two of my house-mates had admitted an attraction to Marta's sister whose name was, and still is spookily, Lucyna. This was irrelevant to me – my target was Marta, and besides, Lucyna was far too tall and spoke little English. (Having said this I don't wish to do her a disservice – she was a great-looking girl, long dark hair with a striking pout).

She was as it happened planning to return to Poland at the beginning of October. In truth she had little choice – she had to finish her last year at university. Marta had decided to stay in England for the time being, not having too many restrictions about her. This I felt was good news as we developed our relationship. I also realised that once gone, Lucyna would leave Marta alone in a large room. "What if I were to move in and keep her company and split the rent?" I mused. We could continue to converse in Polish, financially it would make sense, and I could protect her from the randy house-mates living in the rooms around her. One in particular – a dull insolent French lad, even taller that Lucyna, who smelt slightly of garlic, and who had made a few advances in Marta's direction during that summer. I also recall him having a rather unnatural interest in the game of chess. This in my eyes meant he was a threat – at the very least he was a strategist and I couldn't risk being the victim of a checkmate scenario before I'd even moved my bishop into her queen's castle.

Over the summer I had also purchased a lovely new car, or as new as my finances would allow. A large Rover 620, blue in colour. This blue car plays no further part in this narrative – its significance simply confined to the ease of travel we all enjoyed due exclusively to it. I used to ferry the girls around in it like some Rover-sponsored Alfonso. Like I was an extra along with twin air-bags, electric sunroof and a go-faster stripe. Pimp my Poles!

Going back to my proposal to move in with her - it seemed an obvious idea so I put it to her one evening in the local pub as we supped a pint of local ale. She agreed and, following the slightly officious manner of the Head of Department in charge of staff house allocations, we soon became roomies as they say in America.

As September neared its end and Lucyna got ready to leave we threw her a little party in the boozer and it was all emotional and stuff. I bought her a leaving card splattered with all the Polish phrases they had taught me over the weeks and a chocolate wine bottle with a phrase across the middle in icing. 'Myśleże ten chuj jest luźny.' It was a private joke and referred to a chest of drawers in the French lad's room that had a knob hanging off.

When Lucyna finally did leave, the house was bereft of laughter for a while. We, myself and Marta, suddenly became aware of how close we had become. The room seemed larger and our chatter was equally directed. Everything we said demanded a response from the other person. I noticed her dirty washing, her mannerisms, her favourite television channels, even what deodorant she chose to use. A sense of seriousness began creeping around in that room all unseen, like a blind Grim Reaper desperately looking for his lost scythe whilst trying not to wake anyone up. He often failed, for at the end of the day it was a staff house and those floorboards always creaked which is how we all knew when the French lad went for his fortnightly shower.

My birthday fell on October 4th that year as it tends to do most years and I invited Marta to my parents' house to meet the family. We had a birthday tea and listened to some heavy metal in my old room. I remember Marta bought me a CD. It was Pantera's 'Reinventing Hell'. As a joke (I hoped) she also bought me some Werther's Originals. When questioned on this she just said that as I was now 32 years of age I must now qualify for some – she had some queer idea that they were eaten by old folk? So she had a sense of humour too! We stayed up most of that night talking and listening to Pantera, Iron Maiden and Acid Drinkers. The following morning I felt a little worse for wear but was pleased to see Marta snoring in the spare bed in the spare bedroom. My parents were sticklers for protocol.

That day I took myself off on a short holiday with a few mates to Weymouth. It had been booked for a while and the weather was still alright for early October. But I was mortified at the prospect of a week without my Polish princess. How was I to survive?

During that week I discovered that there was no going back – I was committed here and I wanted this girl. I missed her terribly and the girls on Weymouth beach did little to arouse my ardour. I lost my appetite too on that vacation, so much so that I was afflicted with constipation. (We're back to my brother again!) I went a whole week without going. Actually I tell a lie – I went once on the first night, but that was only because I was alone in a big dark hotel room and watching a particularly scary horror movie.

I've detailed several instances here of my falling for this girl, and I make no apologies for it. It might seem like I'm dramatizing a trivial matter but is love that trivial? Who can deny her when Love comes knocking? I was wooing her and she had to be mine. I concurred with William Shakespeare5 here for I was like a desperate Touchstone stalking his Audrey.

Having said that I'm not about to trivialise it more than is necessary. There are limits to what you can digest so early on in the book. All good writers should be aware of this. Proust6 is a prime example. Had he taken this advice I might've persevered with him a little longer. My 'Remembrance of Things Past' is quick to recollect that Proust was obviously a very bored individual with a propensity for insomnia.

I might toss and turn half a dozen times during the night but, unlike Proust's, my nocturnal manoeuvrings are rarely, if ever noteworthy. They are mostly, I would say, caused by my wife's knee nudging itself (sometimes quite violently should she be having a night terror) into my exposed groin.

I also concede that locating the bedside lamp at three in the morning is in itself a burden, and may even cause said lamp to topple off the dresser, resulting in an expletive (in Polish) from my wife and an accompanying one (English equivalent) from me.

There is another – a sexual realignment may also occur mid-sleep. I often like to nuzzle into my wife as she faces away from me so that the foetal position is adopted. Sometimes, if I'm roused enough from my dreams, I'm not afraid to say, sex happens. Though if it doesn't I at least know that she hasn't left for the spare bed due to my breaking wind or incessant tossing and turning. It's comforting. And not necessarily Freudian.

I could go in this vein but not, thankfully I suspect, for 30 pages. Proust was a pillock and had far too much time on his hands.

CHAPTER THREE

FLOREAT

And here it did so begin to flourish. To bloom, to blossom. It was autumn but the season made no difference to me – I was invigorated. October was as it turned out quite a busy month for me. I had a wedding to attend towards the end of the month and I had promised Marta I would take her to see Whitesnake in Portsmouth the week before. I had always loved the soft velvety voice of Coverdale, and as luck would have it, Marta confessed to liking the band too. With this in mind we took ourselves off to Portsmouth, to the Guildhall to be precise. It was mid-October and the leaves were falling from the trees and the wind swirling them around our ankles as we trudged through the streets towards the venue. We had both elected to wear our 'skóry' which is a Polish term for leathers. Old leather jackets that had been bought years before – I had bought mine as I recall from a market stall around the Tricorn (no mention of Portsmouth would be complete without a reference to the Tricorn) pulled down in recent years to make way for more commercial and perhaps prettier shops, cafes, and bars.

We had a couple of beers first before we went in for the concert. Suitably dressed, I think we even had our 'Motorhead' tee-shirts on as well, we took our seats above the stage. Although not at eye-level we were so close that we were able to see the wrinkles on David's rock-weathered face. He sounded great and the place was soon rocking away to the many tunes of Whitesnake. Marta loved it and I felt a new sense of life to have found a girl that wanted to do this as much as I did. The noise at intervals was incredible, from the band and the crowd. They were clapping to the slower songs, head-banging to the rockier ones, generally getting into the vibe and soaking up the atmosphere. I felt that this was a precursor to later adventures I might have with Marta. And, lo I was to be proved right. By the end of the set we were both pretty exhausted and the support act weren't bad either – The Quireboys – check those guys out. We bought two tee-shirts of the night which we still have to this day and which I still wear from time to time. After a night-cap in a local pub across the road we decided to grab a taxi to a nearby hotel which I had previously and perhaps secretly enquired about and booked. The Keppels Head near The Hard Interchange. A wondrous place even though our room was on the top floor. They were very good to us and despite it being a somewhat respectable establishment and we had no luggage they saw to our needs with goodwill and discretion. The room had a double bed and in spite of the fact I had spent the night in her room at the staff house, I had not yet had the pleasure of sleeping next to her in a presumed dis-robed manner. I had taken a risk but it was late and a taxi back home would have been wallet-destroying. The signs were good (she was tired) and the odds were in my favour I wagered.

That night though once we had settled down, was a difficult one for me. I found it quite hard to drop off in that big double bed. It was slightly uncomfortable and I couldn't get Coverdale's screaming lyrics out of my head, plus I was curled up next to a beautiful Polish girl and we were both half naked. She apparently had no inhibitions and although there was no porn on TV – there was no TV – we snuggled up to each other in a cosy semi-erotic fashion with me trying my best to seem interested but also trying hard not to seem like a pervert – which was harder than you imagine.

When morning came there was no sense of embarrassment or regret and we sauntered out of that hotel like two proud peacocks. We ate our breakfast across the road and reflected on what a great night it had been, and despite sex not happening it was clear from the indicators of interest I was getting from her, and from my strained erection that it would. Shortly. I felt suddenly like a Venusian Artist.

The next weekend we spent apart for I had to attend the wedding of my cousin, Spencer. Spencer is a couple of years younger than me and had proposed to his lovely bride-to-be Danielle several months previously. I did not elect to take Marta as I believe she had made some alternative plans with friends at the time. So I went alone. It was a windy day that day in late-October and nobody kept their hats on. But again here, as the priest said his bit in church and the music played the Wedding March, I felt I was missing something. Marta. I tried to take my mind off her by attempting to eat the whole evening buffet to myself and chatting up the Australian barmaids, though with no real progress by 11.30pm I gave up. They were obviously lesbians. Spencer looked splendid however in his clobber and the family put on a lovely day. I felt proud to be part of the whole event and smiled as I looked at Nan and Granddad beautifully and correctly dressed up in all their finery.

Shortly after this wedding, on coming back to Marta, we got talking about her country, Poland. In more depth. She spoke very passionately about a country divided so many times over the last 1000 years that I began to feel guilty for wanting to keep her in England with me. Was I denying her the chance to go back and live a life she clearly had in her heart? We began to scatter some seeds and towards November those seeds had been sown. I would visit this far-off place she called home. We booked tickets and Marta began sorting out accommodation and everything else only a woman can know about. She said I had shown her some fun in England and now she wanted to return the favour and show me something different at the same time. I felt excited beyond any comprehension. But first I needed to apply for and obtain my passport which was an adventure in itself. The tale went like this....

I had booked an appointment with the passport office to fast-track everything to avoid any delay which as our visit was fast approaching I did not want to encounter. I left for London on a cloudy morning around 9am. Four hours before my appointment which saw me in the queue with ample time to spare. I waited my turn in the snake winding itself round the floor space of the Victoria building, and eventually was seen by a foreign individual who rubber-stamped my application and completed my documents. I could now travel.

I looked at my watch. It was only 2pm. Time for a beer I thought to contemplate my epic journey – which was to leave from this same place in a couple of weeks, Victoria Coach Station, taking an alarming 22 hours. The time never fazed me though. I would be next to Marta and that was worth any amount of time.

I sent a message to one of my mates who lived in Greenwich, south-east London. Donkey. His actual name is of course not Donkey, that would've been strange and wicked on his parents part. His name is Matthew but over the years he has gone by that particular pseudonym. Possibly inspired by the Shrek movies, we did both like and admire Mike Myers. Anyway, I met Donkey in a pub in Covent Garden and we began to catch up on all the news over several beers. As it happened it was his birthday the following week and we got chatting on how he might come to Fareham to visit his family and friends, for he was, before he moved to London to seek his fame and indeed his fortune, my neighbour. We had grown up together. Though I fear our antics as mentioned with my brother are again the subject of another book and must not concern us overly here. Several beers later after leaving Donkey in Covent Garden around 6pm I made my way to the train station in a taxi. The taxi driver took me to Victoria reasonably fast and I paid the man and turned to go. But as I did so he leaned out of the window and looked at me blankly before offering up the immortal line "cunt!" Within earshot I would say of most people in and around Victoria at that time. Probably the passport office heard the obscenity too I would hazard a guess, as they peered out of Her Majesty's windows from above."That's another one we've denied" one might have uttered to another. "Still, bit harsh – he only spelt his name incorrectly" the reply might've been before quietly closing the windows and going back to their respective mugs of coffee.

I took it from this that the taxi driver was expecting some sort of financial reward on top of the fare I had already paid him. Though to be honest it wasn't really an expletive designed to achieve such a result, more to hurt my feelings and alienate me from him thus denying himself the chance of ever getting an extra 80p. The fare was £9.20 and I had handed over a tenner and waited while he shuffled out the change. That was all I had and I wanted to use the toilet at the train station. And I knew that if I had to wait an hour or so four visits to the toilet would've been sufficient given the amount of alcohol I had just put away. Probably. My brain was working fiscally and economically. Shame it gave up on me on the train when I did catch it.

I caught the train back to Fareham around 8pm and arrived back around 2am in the morning with Marta wild with worry. A journey which should have taken 90 minutes took nearly 6 hours! For some reason (the booze in Covent Garden) I fell asleep as we pulled out of Victoria and remained asleep till the train stopped in a run-down little hell-hole called Pokesdown near Christchurch in Bournemouth. Sorry to the inhabitants of Pokesdown, I'm sure it is a nice enough place but at 1 o'clock in the morning it resembled Hell. I cursed and questioned myself. "What am I going to do now? How am I going to get home? Why didn't the train conductor nudge me awake? Did he not want to punch my ticket? Who was a cunt now?"

I made my way through the dark streets of Pokesdown and eventually found a small pizza place open wherein I called Marta, found a cash-point and withdrew 100 pounds which was all I had. The next taxi driver who took me back to Fareham was a jovial sort and did not expect any kind of tip, but just took 90 quid off me as he dropped me off outside the hotel at about 1.50am! I should've let that London taxi driver keep the tenner. That must be what you call karma'd knowledge. They had the knowledge, I didn't. Perhaps on reflection and in light of everything, I was just a cunt.

And so our plans for Poland continued to develop. We were to visit Wrocław, her university city, the mountains in the south, Poznan, her home town Góra and many other places Marta said I should see. I had no idea what to expect having never been abroad apart from a day trip to France, a week in Wales and numerous trips to the Isle of Wight! Her family spoke no English and a panic attack ensued. Marta though, convinced and assured me she would look after me. And to her credit she did just that.

We did everything on that bucket list and more. After landing in the city of Wrocław after 22 hours of monotony interspersed with several showings of Troy on the DVD player, I trod upon Polish soil for the first time. I met Lucyna once again and was introduced to her family and friends. Wrocław was a huge mother of a city, war-torn as it was and had been, its redevelopment had begun and was ongoing. The old buildings in every style imaginable - Gothic, Neoclassical, Baroque - mixed it up with more modern offerings like McDonald's, KFC and strip joints. It is a university city and teems with students and the night-life just exudes energy. It was, I remembered thinking a mini-London. I was immediately struck with the lack of any urgency though. Nobody appeared to be in a rush – not like London. The vibe of the place captured me and holds me to this day. Transport seemed not only to work all the time (something we can't always say of England) but was cheap and continuously available. Even through the night. I had never experienced anything so free as this before. A sense of spreading your wings and being lifted out of the rat-race and let loose... (I lived in Fareham). Whatever you wanted appeared on tap, night or day. We went out several times to see rock bands and drink with friends and caught night buses at 4am back to our hotel. Sometimes Marta would show me little tricks to avoid paying on the buses or the trams, little deceptions that I picked up on and used sporadically over the years when I saw fit. For I was sometimes a cheeky lad!

One day we went with Lucyna to see the group Acid Drinkers in Warsaw. A four hour train journey from Wrocław. This was to become notable not just for the band rocking the club away – Proxima in a back street of Warsaw – but also for our first kiss. We were on the train heading into the capital with out little bottles of Polish stomach vodka, orange in colour, and I leant over towards Marta and went with the words "I want to kiss you but I don't know the words in Polish." It was cheesy and embarrassed Lucyna but it got the job done. I kissed the girl. Then saw the band. Then met the band for autographs – which pleased Lucyna as she had held a torch for the lead singer 'Titus' for a while since the early nineties. Watching this band was to become a part of nearly every trip to Poland over the next few years and as a result we all got to know the members and spoke to them, drank with them, and laughed with them. It was as if we were in the band ourselves. They were and are famous in Poland but fame has not gone to their heads and they remain to their fans at grass roots level. Catch them on YouTube and you may see me thrashing my little head to the heavy beat of the drum and screaming casual obscenities into the crowd.

I ate many new and weird looking concoctions in Poland especially at Marta's home in Góra. Deep in the heart of rural south-west Poland lies Góra, a somewhat forgotten ex-German town, still showing signs of German occupation and brutality. It sits roughly south of Poznan, another large city much like Wrocław. The population is about 12,000, so it's small. Compared to Fareham. Though compared to Wrocław most towns and cities in England are small – its population being nearly 700,000. Góra is like a fish-bowl. Swimming is allowed and encouraged but pretty soon you are going to bump the side of that bowl. You can walk its diameter in 20 minutes or so. Consequently everyone knows everyone else. It has a real community spirit which over time I came to love.

To begin with in Góra it was hard. Marta's parents spoke no English but I felt welcome and began over the months to build a connection. They knew I was trying hard to read and learn Polish and respected me for that. I like to think they came to look upon me as a son to them.

Towards the end of this magical little holiday it snowed. Most of Eastern Europe was blanketed. Our journey back to England through the cold stuff was idyllic. The old huts, the cafes, the bars, the petrol stations, the money exchanges, they were all significant in some way. Because I was sharing them with this wonderful example of womanhood. And I wanted more. Much more. Poland on this first visit showed me a direction, a new way of living, it revived me, woke me up, whatever you want to call it. An epiphany if you like was had. A realisation of something. I wanted to start doing things for us. We spoke about moving in to our own place together back home, and sharing more time together. And I wanted this. I thought if I had someone to share life with that would be great, someone to sleep with even better. And if I could get into her heart as well as her knickers it would certainly have been a job well done.

CHAPTER FOUR

IN ARCADIA

From this moment on things moved into an idolised utopia for me and I rather hope for Marta too. We were practically spending all our free time together as well as working together and boredom never reared its proverbial head. I had worked out the Polish for "can we shag now?" and as we were now sleeping in the same room (hers) I had seen and inadvertently felt her top half. And I can say without any doubt that they both looked and felt great.

As we neared Christmas of that year a new girl moved into the staff house next door. A girl also from Poland – the next batch - and also funnily enough called Marta. A few more may pop up during the course of this epic so if the name is starting to irk you already I suggest you stop reading or go and lie down with a nurofen every chapter or two. I shall instruct someone to draw a red triangle on the top of the page whenever this new Marta is approaching in the narrative.

Red triangle – New Marta was much like us really in where she stood politically and musically – she liked rock music and metal and all things black. Including people – she wasn't racist.

We all got on well in that house of Polish iniquity.

Using my new Rover 620 (alright I mentioned it twice) we all started to hang out and it was around this time that my Marta developed a taste for Primark. (As I imagine a lot of ladies do eventually). The nearest outlet was I think in Portsmouth and this became a place of worship for Marta over the next few years and beyond. In the car I could now take her to places of spectacular interest. Like the upcoming trip to Hounslow!

Christmas felt so new and romantic with Marta and as we made our preparations and bought the gifts and the tree we felt and I sensed that I had entered this for the long haul. Red Triangle New Marta popped round on a daily basis and we chatted in Polish, such was the speed at which I began to pick up the language – and criticised all things British! The staff house at that time had started to lapse into a drunken Roman orgy of debauched madness.

Marta did what she could to make the festive break seem at least a little bit Polish. She cooked up some traditional dishes and we began to speak of what her family would be doing at this time. Perhaps it was me but for the first time I felt as though she was missing Poland slightly more than she was outwardly letting on. With Red Triangle from next door we would often slump into the sofa and drink and smoke and speak obscenely of the world and its foibles. Through the naughty fug of sobriety we remained conscious of the time of year and paid ostentatious respect to Him who died so long ago so that we may guzzle our Carlsberg and puff on our White Ladies. Thank you Lord for surely we are sinning. None of us is wholly good I recanted.

On New Years Eve we drove (myself and Marta) up to Hounslow near Heathrow Airport to see some mates of Marta. Rafal and Monika. Polish friends she'd known for several years. This was the first time that I began to see that drinking to excess could have a negative impact on how I ran my life. Which up until that point or year had been like a saint, save a few minor indiscretions not particularly noteworthy. Monika cooked a gourmet. A feast – of course it was veritable – I don't need to chuck that particular phrasal cliché in there. It just was.

The following day I awoke in a stupor feeling very bloated and windy and no amount of 'Wind-Eze' was going to shift this aggressive indisposition.

In hindsight it was foolish to have agreed to work on New Years Day. But agree I had done. Work, however I did not. Indeed could not. Monika called in sick for me at 1pm. My shift started at 2pm. The boss whose name was Marc was not that happy though he was rather lenient with me at work whenever I erred on the wrong side of things. He took this stance because I supported the same football team as he did. Millwall. South-east London. Though of course at first I had to prove it by showing off my tattoo of the club badge that adorns my upper right arm. This was soon to be something that rendered our relationship binding and was a firm strand of connectedness. I remember him well. A real man's man. Not quite a caveman but not in any sense a modern new-age man

13

(whatever that may be.) Perhaps you know that model, 'The Ascent of Man' where man starts his evolutionary journey as a mere ape and over time, thousands of years obviously, arrives at 'civilised man' rather who we are today. Able to put the kettle on for example. Marc was very much in the middle of that model. The half-crouching-half-standing figure. Some of the things he said were brilliant and oddly poignant of times past – when sexism were rife and Savile and Glitter were in their heyday. I'm not saying that those two scoundrels were alright but at least we didn't have ISIS. Swings and roundabouts. I recall once we were pouring coffee for about a hundred delegates from some big important firm, PriceWaterHouse or Ernst and Young ring some bells, and Marc just stopped mid-pour and looked at me with an anguished look upon his face and uttered a line I still find funny to this day. And to be honest I still use occasionally for comedic effect.

"Gaz" (for he called me Gaz) "I just want to fuck all women!"

He was a great guy. Some people said he might be gay, kind of covering up his real personality, keeping everything in the closet, but he could never be. He hadn't got to that stage during his ascent of man. He used the word 'fuck' in virtually every sentence he spoke – even to senior managers. "This is a fucking shit job Gaz, pouring coffee for these fuckers – lets hurry up and get the fuck home, I don't give a fuck anymore!"

His use of this derogatory word didn't impress me at the time but it did later. I once held a short conversation lesson in Poland entirely based on the word 'fuck' and its many different uses with regard to grammar and parts of language.

As a noun - "I had a great fuck last night"

As a verb - "To fuck or not to fuck"

As an adjective - "He's a fucking idiot"

Even a gerund - "Before fucking I leave work"

And so on in that vein.

Anyway once the New Year had arrived I took myself and Marta up to Bexleyheath to visit my Nan and Granddad. They always showered me with affection and love and showed an interest in me and what I was up to. Money was thrown more often than not in my direction and I felt an affinity with these two old people and they became over the years a massive influence on me. They were typical grandparents and were always there for me and the rest of the family with a shoulder to cry on or moan on, or whatever. And always with a cup of tea and a biscuit beside a roaring fire in their front room.

On this occasion they fed us till our belts or skirts needed attention and gave us 100 pounds to spend in London. So we went 'up-west.' I shelved out on a new pair of brogues and treated Marta to a lovely Italian meal just off The Strand near Charing Cross. Our waiter that day was a Polish guy called Marcin who was adequately impressed with my fumbling Polish that he bought us both drinks. Again the beginnings of an epiphany. I started to notice that these people were more than ready to do things for me, and I liked it. I didn't always get what I wanted at home and my parents were great at instilling that work-ethic in me. You can achieve anything you want but you have to work for it. I felt sometimes that they always had their eye on me watching what I was up to especially once I left school, eager of course for me to do well in life. All well and good and this motivated me no end but love without effort sometimes had its place too. Like in that Charing Cross restaurant – or at my Nan's house. I was a happy child of course though prone to bouts of enforced melancholy. (Whenever my parents forced me to watch Coronation Street!) But as Tolstoy once said "every family is unhappy in its own way."

Around the end of January 2005 our hotel held a party for staff and their guests. Marta and I attended and proceeded to eat and drink the evening away. During a mid-party raffle our number came up and we won a dinner for two at a local 5-star hotel. I don't know whether this piece of good fortune on our part initiated a pang of jealousy amongst our cohorts or what it was, but shortly after the raffle things took an ominous turn. It was a typically raucous affair anyway as those parties always used to be, but by 11pm I heard that a series of drunken scuffles had broken out which had culminated in several fully-fledged fights.

Happily we had left by this time and were tucked up in bed celebrating our 5-star culinary win in predictable fashion.

The next month we visited Poland again. This time the snow was in for the duration. Wrocław, Marta's university city, was once again blanketed.

Ah, Wrocław – my utopian dream-world. Marta studied, lived and worked within its great expanding heart of beauty. Formerly of course, Breslau, the German name, here was a place that was to become a big part of my life over the next few years.

Wrocław thrives on tourism now but it has a beating heart that sets it apart from other places I have been to. It seems to exist not just because it is there but because it lives just like you or I. It is an entity with a pulse and a character. A huge population as noted, some 700,000 gives it a vibe, a personality and several mojos to boot. It didn't take long for me to become transfixed.

In Marek Krajewski's7 'Phantoms of Breslau' set in 1919, the protagonist Eberhard Mock interprets the city as a deeply sinister yet beguiling metropolis. A place where over the decades good and evil have been artistically woven from the same palette. Thankfully unlike Mock in 1919 I never once encountered a series of badly beaten and/or mutilated dead bodies within the confines of this sprawling Leviathan. But I did, like him, allow myself to be romanced and thrilled by the goods on offer. (Not alone I must add – I was always with Marta and/or friends). The seedy drinking-dens, the underground drug-hideouts, the smoke-laden strip-joints, they were all atriums or ventricles of the city's throbbing heart.

Krajewski's 'Phantoms' are a part of Wrocław but there is so much more.

During this visit we also went to see another 'Acids' gig. We had front row tickets next to the speakers! Marshall Stacks became my friend for life that night. I had my photo taken with the guitarist whose name was 'Olass' and familiarity between us began to sprout green shoots of life.

At that time before contractors came in and redeveloped vast swathes of land and open space within the city, Wrocław was awash with tiny wooden shacks or sheds. Everywhere they used to be, on every street corner, every road, every pathway. Situated willy-nilly, as they were, you could buy whatever you liked from ice-cream, sweets or snacks to newspapers, toys or photographic equipment. We used to love eating something called 'Rurki z Kremem' or small wafer tubes filled with fresh cream. At about 15p for one and with English money in our respective wallets we filled our boots. Which was good because it made a change from them being filled with snow!

Sadly these places have largely died out or have become fewer and farther between. Poland has had immense investment over the last 10 years and commerce is now the way to go. Disregarding value or use to the community if it was small and didn't make much money it could be replaced with a vast shopping mall or a hotel etc. That was probably the thinking. Shame. In 2004 and 2005 the commercial juggernaut was coming but had not yet hit. The brakes had been applied through sporadic anti-western protests or communism clingers-on, though ultimately to no avail. Nothing was going to stop the 'Coca-Cola truck' hitting and shedding its western-based commercial load.

We found a lovely English pub in the centre of town called, quite nationally, 'John Bull.' Its style was indeed that of Old Blighty. Slightly discoloured beer-stained carpets, a piano in the corner, glass tankards hanging above the bar and prints of famous English battles upon the walls. It also showed football on two giant screens. I would often frequent this pub in times of reverie and think of folk back home and what they all might be up to. Whenever I head back to Poland even now I stride straight for this lovely little place, such is its allure.

You used to be able to buy this cheap wine in Poland called 'Gull.' Perhaps the equivalent of 'Lambrini' here, it was sold in various off-licences and came in several flavours. It was what you drank if you were either a student or a homeless piss-head on the street. One night Lucyna invited us to her 'Halls of Residence' where she was staying whilst studying at university. Along with about 10 other students and friends we congregated in a corridor and began what can only be described now as a mess! Students can drink a bit and to keep pace with them I downed two bottles of this 'Gull' which I think was blackcurrant in flavour. Not content with this I also managed several beers as well which brought on the brightest red nose I have ever had to this day! I have very little memory of that night but I slept like a coffin-based resident! This was one of the first times I realised that it was foolish to try and keep up with Polish drinking people. Though it wasn't to be the last.

The next day, once recovered we went to the 'Panorama Racławicka' a quite exemplary circular museum depicting a famous victory for the Polish peasants and army against those pesky marauding Russians. 'Kościuszko' was and is of Nelson's ilk. For any visitors to Wrocław this place is a must-see. The museum itself is in the middle of a park right in the centre of town. Entrance is around a fiver for an adult. Inside is a painting that stretches dozens of metres around you as you stand in the middle. The artwork alone is tremendous. The painted scenes show Kościuszko and his peasant army fighting against the invading Russians. Soldiers, women, children, priests, horses and weaponry all clearly and meticulously drawn. Headphones allow translations as the explanations are of course in Polish. Hang me if it doesn't bring a tear to your eye.

We also got the train to Poznan, a city similar in size to Wrocław, to meet a tailor who made leather gear for Acid Drinkers. Lucyna had his number from 'Titus' the lead singer from the band and we fixed a date. He produced a pair of strides for me that looked every inch 'rock-star' and an inch or two homosexual! They had a flag on each buttock. An English one on the left and a Polish one on the right! My dual identity had cemented itself. On my arse.

Poznan is a delightful city too, though perhaps more business-oriented than Wrocław. We sampled something called 'Zapiekanka' which we were led to believe was a local speciality. It was like a pizza-slice but all of two-feet long! We ate it laboriously together Lady and the Tramp style.

The weeks and months went by as I slowly became more entrenched with my new-found Polish identity. More Polish people moved into the staff house and started work. Marta was happy as she had more folk to talk to using natural repartee. Pawel, a pot-wash guy from middle Poland was notable as he seemed a likeable bloke, mid-forties perhaps, a little dirty in mind and body but with a cracking daughter, Agata. A blonde shell of a bomb not unlike Britney Spears. Pawel was not a handsome man by any stretch of the imagination but this girl did not seem to have his 'John Merrick' hereditary genes. Despite this Pawel would join us regularly on our 'Beavis and Butthead' futon, drinking and smoking and generally putting the world to rights.

Things went on like this until May of that year when we made a decision that shook me to the core. A new fear began to bubble within me - mostly in my underpants – as we embarked upon booking plane tickets to Poland on May 28th. Never before had I flown. Planes, heights were a big no-no for me. I didn't do them. Simply. We are not birds, we don't have wings, we shouldn't fly. And no good can come of it. That was always my view. And to a degree still is.

Having taken a trip to the airport by coach the night before we proceeded to plonk ourselves down and try for some kip. Awkward at 11pm at Stansted Airport. Our flight was early next morning around 8am I believe so that meant we had around 7 or 8 hours to wait. Time, ample, I thought to prepare myself for this life-changing avionic adventure.

Time passes slowly when you're sat on a plastic seat with nothing to do but listen to the faint sound of far-off chatter, or the hum of the cleaning machines whirring up and down the airport aisles willy-nilly. Time itself slows down.

Eventually after several sleepless hours had passed and I had wandered countless times around including a few stops off at the pub for confidence, night gave way to dawn. Richard Whiteley had stopped the clock with a resounding 'duh-duh, duh-duh, duh-duh duh duh, boom' that I was sure half of Essex could have heard!

My fear grew with every ticking second. My world view, comfortable and warm was about to be shattered. Just 12 hours ago I was sat at home with Red Triangle Marta and Pawel laughing and watching 'The Weakest Link' on television. Chuckling, as I was, at Anne Robinson's wink, which I have always found to be both evil and horrifyingly sexy. She gives off misleading signals that woman. She displays an air of irritability no matter the occasion, much like, as Sue Townsend once said in Adrian Mole, Harriet Harman the labour politician does. These types of women might be right dirty in bed but they will metaphorically destroy you shortly after the bedroom encounter.

I felt also an M R James8 'Mezzotint' situation coming on. An eternally changing picture where nobody can understand what is happening nor see the outcome. It got so that I was afraid at what every new step would bring. What I thought was correct was now being slowly and methodically taken away leading to an indescribable fear which I calculated could only be Death, of a kind. A fate as yet unknown like Dante9 leading Virgil down through those nine circles of Hell. "Where do I want to get off?" I pondered.

The Departure Lounge? The toilets? The newspaper stand? The Coffee Shop? (It was Starbucks so I think I disregarded that particular station. Better Death than such Dishonour!) But in reality there was no getting off. Sitting on that plane for me would represent the deepest, darkest pit of Hell. The lowest circle of Dante's satanic excursion, which is I believe Treachery.

17

Once on the plane itself I began to wish I'd stopped with Virgil at Limbo or Lust. Gentle chastising and/or casual flagellation might have been more appealing than what I was about to experience. At least, I thought, were I blindfolded, I could have imagined it was Anne Robinson applying the cat o' nine tails, straight from Hell and all that, whist Harriet Harman stood naked barking instructions to Robinson as she winked at each crack of the whip. Thinking about that now, hellish though that vision undoubtedly was, there was also nothing Satan could have done to stop it being simultaneously slightly erotic.

As time moved swiftly on at a pace I was completely uncomfortable with and ignoring all my Deathly reverie, I turned to see on the boards above that our plane had landed and was now ready to turn around and head back to Poland. My heart suddenly began to beat on the outside of my body.

CHAPTER FIVE

POST NUBILA, PHOEBUS

After two or perhaps three vodkas which helped me board this flying bus we shuffled along the cabin and located our seats. A pang of fear shot through me as I realised there was nowt I could do to get out of this situation. The seat-belts were fastened, and the luggage safely packed away into the overhead lockers. Presently and almost without warning the plane slowly taxied along the runway towards take-off. The fun had at the airport now forgotten as we became locked within this capsule about to launch us into the clouds. Then the engines roared with aggression as we attained the speed required to lift us off the ground. Shooting down the runway into certain death, I thought. Then as if God Himself had reached out a hand and scooped us into His holy palm, our plane left the ground!

The hours spent at the airport forgotten as our Boeing 737 soared into the clear morning sky. As we climbed ever higher I think I even prayed. Once we levelled out though at 30,000 feet, I realised that if we were going to die here there was nothing I nor anyone else could do about it, so I decided to have another couple of in-flight beers. £2.80 for a small can of Heineken. I wasn't going to sniff at that, having more pressing things to worry about. Price of beer was the last thing on my mind at that point.

There were, perhaps unsurprisingly no strange occurrences in the sky that day and we flew to our destination without incident. Landing was OK. I could see all the buildings and the countryside getting bigger and this was a source of comfort, oddly enough. Then presently, after nearly two hours, our wheels bumped the ground and everyone clapped. This has always struck me as odd. As if a round of applause is needed for landing safely. For averting a disaster. It's the norm isn't it? To land. To fly, take off and land. Why the incessant clapping? It would be like driving my car to work and on parking in the relevant bay seeing all of my work-mates gather round and shower me with praise, their applause masking their affectations. "The lad did well, now back to work."

We took many photos in Poland this time but I think the trip was momentous because of seeing Iron Maiden, my all-time favourite rock group play in Katowice, southern Poland. We got tickets and found our way right on top of the band a few metres away from the stage. Myself, Marta and her younger sister Ada, together with Lucyna, her new boyfriend Remko, a Dutch guy, and a friend of his over for a holiday. Our respective ears were throbbing for two hours or more and Maiden blew the other bands away that day, which was not that hard as they were mediocre at best. Though Nightwish were on form. What a voice!

We also went to the mountains in the south on the Polish-Czech border. We scaled the highest peak, a mountain called 'Snowball' some 1600 metres above sea-level. Part of the ascent we had chosen to conquer in a rickety old chair-lift that creaked and groaned with every breath. My life was in the balance once again! But at the top as we crossed into the Czech Republic the view took all of my remaining breath away! The steep inclines and slopes were even blanketed in snow in some parts near the top! In June!

At the bottom we stayed in a Swiss-style chalet, near the foot of the mountain, and at £25 for three nights, well do I need to explain? The gang had a ball, as the Yanks would say. Many a local pub was sampled, and all open most of the night!

We met other relatives on this trip including some cousins, aunts and uncles and a dear old grandma. Marta's grandma, Maria. She was around 85 and typical of what you might imagine a grandma from a deep rural part of Poland might be like. Flowery dresses and skirts, hair bedraggled, snaggle-toothed perhaps, but blessed with all the traditions and customs of old. A Polish matriarch. And she loved her family. She spoke often in a language that was hard to understand even for her family – language that had been forgotten, words and phrases that perhaps no longer existed or had changed in usage. It would always make us smile as we sat over the years in her lounge drinking tea and munching on all the food she continued to trudge out with which to compliment the Polish dinner table.

This visit also coincided with Lucyna's birthday and we decided to celebrate in a pub called 'From Dusk Till Dawn' in Wrocław, and so invitations were sent out.

I love this pub. Simply love it. It plays heavy metal music and heavy rock. From time to time they also feature famous bands too. Its interior consists of brickwork with many objects emerging from the walls, things like an American police-car, a speed-bike and so on! It's like the Musee d'Orsay for people who may be partial to Ozzy Osbourne. It is situated about ten minutes walk from the town square, and is below the ground, as a lot of pubs and bars are in Wrocław. Many were simply underground labyrinths during the war. Bolt holes for escapees or German troops. Another reason for the vibe I talked of earlier. It's eerie. But enlightening. We had a huge cake in this pub as Lucyna partied away dancing and rocking into the wee small hours.

The main square just teemed with life, day and night. I had never known anything so beautiful as this before. Fareham is never going to be European City of Culture, is it? I do know however that Wrocław will hold this title and have this honour in 2016.

We endured or survived many more parties over the next few days or so, including a party at another student accommodation Marta knew. She was friendly with the receptionist lady who was about 50 years old. I think she knew her as she used to stay there when studying herself. This lady's name was Jadwiga. We met a few students around 8pm one evening and just continued to talk and laugh. During which time several more students joined us and the next thing we knew it was about 6am! My Polish improved no end that night.

The two weeks we spent this time in Poland went by so quickly and soon we were on our way back to the airport to fly back to Stansted. We managed to scrape a lift to the airport from friends Marta knew (she has so many pals!) called Ryba and Kasia. Two great people. Ryba, whose name in English means fish, was a fantastic bloke, who could contort his face into many different shapes. Like a jelly mould. He's a funny guy and will do anything for you. Also he is a pretty big guy physically and, as I found over the following few years, on occasion, he is a great man to have around when faced with potential threats from fellow drunken thugs. Yes, they do exist in Poland and they tend to be bigger than they are in the UK. It's the constant food barrage from the snaggle-toothed grandmas feeding them up!

I was OK on the return flight. I flew with comparative ease. As we landed and made our way out through the airport I caught sight of the seats we had sat on two weeks ago. Now occupied by other souls, a bit nervy, a bit stressed, a bit tipsy. Who knew?

We boarded a coach back to Fareham – a sad but more cultured man was I.

A couple of weeks after this Ada, Marta's younger sister, came over to see us in Fareham. We spent our days visiting local hotspots and sampling English food. She liked living with us and tried her best to understand the way of life here. We joked as you would expect with all the staff house folk and smoked a little 'naughty sofa-tobacco.'

September of that year saw us fly off to Holland to see Lucyna and Remko who had invited us over for a few days. We flew EasyJet as prices were a bit cheaper and we could fly from Gatwick. My nerves were not under complete control but they were better than the trip to Poland previously. I tried bravado on the plane to show how strong and brave I was by chatting up this Polish air-stewardess. Her name was Asia and she was quite impressed with my language skills. Marta however, was less impressed.

Holland proved to be an eye-opener. A 50-minute flight and we touched down in Schiphol international airport to be greeted by the guys again. Marta's other sister Ola was also there with her new bloke Pepe, from Spain. Ola is the second oldest after Marta and at that point was living and working in Spain. Marta has three sisters and it seemed to me at the time that theirs was a very multi-national family with siblings spread out across Europe as they were.

Remko took us to some of the local places of interest. Bars and cafes and seedy little drinking dens. He lived in Utrecht, a city about 30 minutes from Amsterdam – Holland is rather small though and to be honest every city or town is around 30 minutes from Amsterdam! We went for a cruise along the canal through Utrecht in small pedal boats and thus began my next foolish adventure...

Lucyna and Remko in one boat started pedalling up-river towards the nearest bridge and a series of small river-side bars. I thought I would go, with Marta in my boat, the other way – down-river. After several minutes I realised that people were shouting at us from the promenade and from the cafes on either side. Of course I had no idea what they were saying so continued my journey down-wind. It was when I caught sight of a pleasure-boat packed with tourists and irate-looking crew that I understood I was pedalling in the wrong direction and that all river-craft was supposed to head in the same direction! Lucyna and Remko were shouting something in the distance as we sailed away from them. I now knew what that was! I felt rather silly and sheepishly started to pedal back the right way, performing a three-point-turn against the current and with the pleasure boat creeping up beside me and all its passengers outwardly mocking me for my show of river stupidity.

The next day Marta got her hair cut for free. I make no apologies for the inclusion of this next anecdote. Everything I write is of course true and these are real tales I tell. Remember that before you go accusing me of homophobia or generalising.

Remko's brother Rody is a raging homosexual. And he's a hairdresser.

A deal was struck between him and this other guy he was trying to impress at the time. I'm sure the deal was "if you cut this girl's hair for free, I will...." (insert your own imaginative construction here).

This guy duly obliged and Marta got her barnet trimmed for no money. Rody left that salon with a smile of expectation etched across his boat, insinuating that come closing time he and his friend would be making sure that the word which meant 'happy, glad and full of life' in the 1970s had now changed its meaning.

Rody always reminds me of that joke. A girl is talking to her friends about babies. "I want three kids" she says. "One of each." "How does that work?" replies another. "Well", says the first girl, "I would like a boy, a girl, and a hairdresser."

Sex was everywhere on that visit. There were bars with girls in bikinis, who danced on the table in front of you offering you more beer for a pound of Dutch flesh, and a quick shake of their thrupennies. There was the sex museum and street walkers and so on. Of course we visited the Red-light District. But such things are expected in Holland, especially Amsterdam, and as noted at the start of this opus, can often be a bit tedious and John Cleland10 I certainly ain't. Despite a decent look around that sex museum I was never able to find mention of that Fanny.

I experienced something else. Remko showed us something which I found truly remarkable and strangely amusing. He drove us to a large industrial site, a sort of oval, which resembled a race track. As you drive along all these women are lined up, track-side, and the idea is that you drive slowly, survey the goods, pick the one you fancy and drive along the track to the other side. Usain Bolt would call this the 200 metre starting point. Here there were many 'parking bays' where obviously you park and do the business. Then when you finish you start the car up again and drive back round to the point at which you came in and rejoin the main road! It's sort of like a pit-stop for discerning gentlemen. It's the strangest race I have ever seen where if you come first you not only leave without a medal but with guilt and shame screaming across your face! And in Holland in that type of race drugs weren't at all scorned upon. Indeed not only were they positively encouraged, Remko said that in some cases they were mandatory!

Back in England Marta and I had a discussion about our future and a decision was made that we would try to fly as often as possible to Poland and for me to try and find a job over there for a while. What prompted this discussion was that she had chosen mid-way through October to go back to Poland to study for a new exam. She looked solemn as she told me that she had had a great time in the little town of Fareham but that the time had now come to move on. The hotel was told of our intentions and Marta handed in her notice. A few tears were shed but I was determined that this would not tear us apart. It would be the start of a new adventure.

On the day she departed I took her to London and we said our goodbyes. Her coach glided out from Victoria and through the dusty streets and out of sight as I waved. Then I sat alone not sure of what to do next. Both the Polish sisters gone. But Marta would not be gone forever. This was a new chapter.

The days following her departure were banal and devoid of laughter. Red Triangle Marta at the staff house offering scant hilarity. The days seemed dull and without sunshine. Ou est le soleil?

To make matters gloomier we received some horrible news. My Nan had been told she had cancer. Of the lungs and elsewhere. It was terminal. She was not expected to live very long. She started treatment but it was a slow and debilitating thing to undergo. She was over 80. My heart was torn again. I wondered if after all the excitement I had had over the last year or so, the maxim could work in reverse.

Post nubila, Phoebus.

CHAPTER SIX

AMOR VINCIT OMNIA

Time moved on very slowly through November and December as we plodded our way through to Christmas. Marta in Poland. Me, stuck as I was in Fareham with not much to keep me occupied other than work. Now would come the test – could love indeed triumph over separation?

On Friday 16th November I left Fareham again for Stansted airport, having booked a flight to see Marta for a few days in Wrocław. As my journey began to unfold I wondered whether after four weeks of separation she would still believe in us as a couple. Perhaps she had found another, more stable interest in Poland and might be about to abort on me. Your mission has been unsuccessful on this occasion! But thoughts like this were distracting me from clarity of mind and I knew from our calls and messages that she at least still valued me as a friend.

I arrived at the airport around 11pm that day. My flight did not depart until the next morning at about 8am. I wanted to get there with plenty of time to spare – something I have proved time and time again to be a wise decision over the years. Perhaps here I do National Express a disservice. They rarely renege on their vows to get the passenger to his destination at the time stated on his ticket. But having checked out their illustrious timetable I discovered that the first bus that morning would have dropped me off at the airport around 7.30am. With approximately 30 minutes to spare before take-off. I felt that too much of a risk. So I sat down on the hard plastic chairs dotted here there and everywhere about the vast airport and tried to drop off myself. I did attempt sleep but it eluded me. The seats uncomfortable and the noise sporadically unbearable, I was fighting a cause which to use the cliché was lost. Then at midnight a strange thing happened. The noise ceased. It became noiseless. A silence hung in the air above us. Nothing happened. No people wandering like each and every one of them was the poor Jew Ahasuerus11. "There's to be no second coming – you are destined to wander forever! Fool that you are!"

No staff. No security personnel. No cleaning machines with moronic-looking zombie drivers atop steering and cleaning to and fro, up and down, leaving trails of water behind like haphazard snails with a sleep disorder. Nothing. Yet despite all this I could not induce sleep. This eerie state of affairs continued for some time till about 3.30am when all at once the front doors opened and in came dozens upon dozens of flying holiday-makers trampling their way to the check-in desks which had suddenly opened up as if by magic. "Excuse me, I'm trying to take a nap here," I silently plead and/or curse. My prayer falls on deaf ears. From 4am there was nothing I could have done to grab a few winks let alone forty, and so I rose and followed the masses and got in a queue to order the earliest breakfast I thought I was ever likely to consume. The Russian or Spanish girl next to me who had been playing ridiculous tunes on her Walkman all night, keeping herself and countless others around her awake, then miraculously fell asleep! How, I could not fathom an answer!

Presently after all the early morning kerfuffle and the boredom had abated I boarded my plane just before 8am and flew quite majestically and with a certain amount of confidence to Wrocław. Then after four weeks we met once more. She came flitting into the arrivals lounge to greet me and we were as one again.

Her new flat she had procured was very nice and she shared it with one of her friends, a shy pretty girl called Magda and three other university girls. All in it was a squeeze – though to be honest sharing a two-bedroomed flat with five beautiful Polish girls wasn't something I was about to argue about! Over the next few days we met everyone again and did the family thing and started to make plans for a potential future in Poland. "Could I work out here?" The question hung in the Polish air like the rain cloud A A Milne12 wrote of. "Was it possible?" pondered I.

Marta showed me around her school where she had been studying for a new exam. The CAE. A beast of an exam. It was during this little impromptu tour that I latched onto the possibility that I might be able to go down this avenue myself. Education. Teaching. Marta knew some friends who were both teachers and school directors and we began to talk tentatively about my prospects. At that time these dreams were just that. Fanciful ideas. I never once believed that I could pull off such an enterprise. I had no experience, and didn't speak enough Polish, and on top of that had various financial quirks that would make it hard for me to leave the UK. But if you are reading this and you know me then you will be aware that ultimately, leave I did.

I concluded at that time that I was happy to spend time out in Poland, hopefully every month or so, which I could do from work with a few clever shift denominations and a very helpful boss, Kylie. (Marc had by then left the fucking hotel for fucking pastures new). She was Australian as I recall, as I suppose she must've been with a name like that. We had a very good working relationship, and I think she came to know that I could discover Ayers Rock, but like the boomerang, I would always come back. She trusted me did Kylie. And I always had a soft spot for her too as to me her name associated itself with a kind girl-next-door type, a delicate voice and a pair of clingy hot-pants.

Marta and I made plans to spend Christmas in Poland that year. It was to be a coach trip as I had a lot of luggage and plane tickets were expensive. I remember taking over lots of gifts for the family in a vain attempt to ingratiate myself further into the folds of Marta's family. They were taken in by my generosity. Though of course it was heartfelt. I also took over some festive English food. Mince pies, Christmas pudding and a few crackers to boot. Her mum laid up a table that Christmas Eve like one of my dad's old wallpapering tables he used to keep in the garage. It was huge and consisted of twelve places relating to the disciples of our good friend Jesus Christ, plus one extra place said to be for anyone who might come a knocking during the evening in need of nourishment. Luckily no-one did and I ate like a flipping horse! That poor homeless man missed out on a grand scale that evening I can tell you. There were so many different courses and they just flowed and I quite got caught up in the tradition of it all. We opened presents and shared rice-paper with one another and wished everybody good luck for the coming year. The open fire threw out a deep orange glow that made everyone seem like Santa himself. Rouged-up cheeks abounded. The Poles celebrate Christmas Eve more than the day after and most of the festivities take place on the 24th. The Church is of course a major player and several pilgrimages were undertaken over the two days. So it was that in these high spirits – though not too high as alcohol is not permitted on Christmas Eve and nobody drank anything - that I did indeed find a way to prove that love could conquer all. Among my gifts from afar, and aside from gold, frankincense and myrrh, was a neat little box with Marta's name on it. And below the towering Christmas tree, as family members looked on with varying degrees of aghastness etched across their Yuletide faces, I pledged my friendship to Marta. And I lied about the alcohol thing – it now occurs to me that I did, with my own trusty seeing-orbs, witness her mum quaff a small glass of liqueur just before 10pm.

CHAPTER SEVEN

QUIS SEPARABIT?

Who indeed? With a ring on her finger albeit without bells on her toes, there was now no doubt that she should have music wherever she goes. My contented heart sang melodiously as I felt for the first time in my life I had something to hold on to. Something precious. And not a Gollum in sight. I suppose at the time we became unofficially engaged as friends and as a couple we pledged our troth to each other.

On New Year's Eve that year we celebrated in style by going to the music festival in the town square in Wrocław. Thousands upon thousands of people also had the same idea and several crushes later we sang and danced our engaged way into 2006. We finally got to bed that morning about 4am and slept with dreams of weddings and horses and carriages invading our very souls. Here then was something to work towards and plan for. Initially we did nothing but as the weeks and months rolled by more and more decisions were made and I began to see my life ebbing and flowing like the tide towards an unknown destination, with I as a mere sailor spectator with a zest for excitement and full of innocent expectation. I was like a European Sinbad the Sailor.

I travelled back from Poland on the 2nd January 2006 and became part of England once again. Whilst out there I was offered a job at a hotel. A hotel where Marta had started to work at a month or so earlier. She was now a housekeeping assistant manager. Her boss, a deeply unnerving man and something big in religion (the hotel was called The John Paul the 2nd Hotel), interviewed me and seemed to take a particular liking for me as a foreign lad. The deal was that I could start after a month and that I could earn around 1000zl a month. Equivalent to about £200. I would be a general assistant and work up the ladder. His words – though in Polish. Marta had reservations. I had more. The money, quite apart from this man who sat grinning at me throughout most of the interview in a very religiously sinister fashion, was the sticking point.

So we chose to say no on that occasion but at least it had given me some valuable experience and so I started to put myself about job-wise in Wrocław.

On the Sunday following my arrival back in Fareham we had the yearly staff party at work. I went along fuelled by the recollection of the previous year's do when I was with Marta and celebrating our free dinner six-nought, whilst those staff house ruffians slugged it out around us. I also went to confirm whether or not any girl would be wearing a bikini. The theme that year was James Bond. I felt sure someone would do an Andress. Sadly no-one did.

It was around this time, early January, that Red Triangle Marta from next door, as you remember, started to pay me more attention both at work and at home. We continued to socialise from time to time and smoked various substances of which in my innocence I knew nothing. One particular evening I must mention. Drug-related it is. I don't really like this particular anecdote for I believe it makes me look less than angelic, which I always strive to be of course. Hold your judgement as I recount what actually happened that evening:

We had been working hard, both of us one cold winter's day in January and had come home and had eaten together. Some lacklustre and meagre offerings no doubt. Tinged with boredom and with the realisation that Eastenders was about to come on, Marta suggested smoking something different 'for a laugh.' We slumped into the sofas and switched off the encroaching televisual torture-flick. "No Phil Mitchell tonight" I gleefully thought inwardly. It must have been around 8pm and to my knowledge we were alone in the house. After a few minutes Marta, adept as she was at rolling, produced something that looked like a small javelin or a hat for a tiny member of the Ku Klux Klan. A member who had obviously strayed into Jonathan Swift's13 Lilliput whilst we, the smokers, held fast to our Brobdingnagian statures. But did we expect to see Laputa? Well, it didn't come that flying island in the sky. Neither did we see any Yahoos or visit the country of the Hounyhnhnms, though we quickly began to lose all devotion to reason. Talking horses I have you! Whatever next? You have to wonder after all this whether in fact Swift was partaking of the same substance that we were about to. Or was he simply a contemporary Ian Hislop?

Anyway as I was saying – we puffed our way though a couple of these javelins, or miniscule KKK hats and in a short while I realised to my amusement that I needed to go to the toilet. Marta was fine. She was Polish and had a bigger bladder. I however needed to get up and visit the boy's room which was situated about two metres away next to me. It was about this time as I fumbled with the folds of the well-worn futon I was embedded within, that I suddenly became aware of a mysterious 'heavy weight' just above my head pushing me downwards back into the sofa. Whether Laputa or not I did not know. I called across to Marta who by now had developed a strange look of grinned contemplation. She looked like a Polish Cheshire cat. I tried again for the toilet but once more the oddly-weighted mass forced me back down. It was after several of these unsuccessful attempts to get up and stumble the aforementioned two metres to the karsey, that, as Marta continued grinning like a feline from Cheshire, I wet myself!

And still I could not move off that frigging sofa. Some time later, minutes or hours, we never formed an opinion on the timescale, I did arise and slinked back to my own room next door. Hiding my shame-sodden wranglers and my stupid drug-addled pride. It certainly was not hubris.

Towards the end of the next month, February, I travelled once more to Wrocław. That winter as I recall was the first time that I had experienced significantly low temperatures. There were days when the mercury recorded minus 25C along with the snow that blanketed most of Poland. A bleak hinterland. I was to meet Lucyna over there this time and we of course renewed our friendship. Remko provided all things jocular as expected. We went to what was fast becoming my favourite underground pub in Wrocław. 'From Dusk Till Dawn' in the town centre. Heavy metal and girls in black leather. Who needs Gulliver's mysterious potions? This was the high I had craved for. Towards the end of February Marta introduced me to her friend, Iza, who worked in a local School of English. I went in to impress with my developing language and my love for Poland. She recommended a course that she said might be of some assistance to me in England if I was serious about going down the teaching route. TEFL courses and short classes were mentioned. Either way I had decided to channel my energies into English teaching influenced as I was by several comrades of Marta who had done the same thing. Should I fail then my thinking was that I may have to ask Marta to come back to the UK to make a go of things. Something I didn't really want to do. Poland, due to my many trips, was quickly becoming a new home for me. I was slowly beginning to realise that at the same time as I was relishing each jaunt, it too was reaching its arms out to me and beckoning me into its genteel warmth. All traditional and all.

One other event that opened my eyes a bit more around this time was the evening we went to a huge disco in a city called Leszno, close to Góra where Marta's parents lived. I suppose it is situated about 80 kilometres from Wrocław. A somewhat smaller city with a population around 70,000, I would liken it to Fareham without its Stubbington/Gosport/Titchfield tentacles. Central to this city is a quaint old town-hall with a clock tower which chimes out hourly bongs along with a traditional Polish melody every hour on the hour.

This disco was a normal disco. Lights, strobes and lazers and all you would expect of such a shin-dig. Not really my cup of rosy but since Marta and some friends were going and more contacts were needed I went along. Amazingly Marta also invited her parents! And Remko and his dad tagged along too. It was a family disco it seemed. Never in a million years would I ever have considered taking my parents to a Fareham disco! The shame. Wetting my trousers again would have been more appealing. Dads fix bikes and cars. Mums do the washing and the shopping. They do not throw shapes to DJ Jazzy Mushroom Decks and his exploding upbeat techno sounds! Marta's parents and Remko's dad however embraced this event by kicking their legs and flinging their arms around like they were having some kind of melodic stroke or something. It was fun. And my thoughts on my own family doing the same were rendered silly in the face of this full-on assault by this highly irregular, as I then thought, disco-balled situation. The Poles, as I came to learn, had no inhibitions. The English, as I came to realise had some. I danced at that disco till about 4am. Myself and Marta and Ada hit the floor moving with the crowds, twisting our minds and bodies in equal measure to the mesmerising din.

I was rediscovering myself. I slowly managed to do more things on my own. One day whilst Marta was at work I went to see that old mate of hers who worked at a local hostel for students. That lady called Jadwiga. A single lady. I tried to engage her in conversation and did so for nearly two hours. A growing sense of hubris once again. We had a few interesting times with this lady – who Marta had met whilst a student herself. Jadwiga was a lovely lady. To the students that stayed in her hostel she was both aged and of a different age. She had witnessed the fall of Communism. Whilst not ever sympathetic to it, she remained in tune with its poetic significance. I smiled as I recalled that party with her once. Some students started to drink in the foyer, the lobby area, refusing to sign or check themselves back in after a drunken day-drinking session no doubt. Jadwiga first tried to reason with them, but very briskly gave up on this and proceeded to procure more drink, and lo and behold we all pulled up chairs and drank till way past midnight! With Jadwiga. I never saw CCTV. I was a hit. The students all appeared interested in me and my lame attempts to speak their language, which seemed to come on in leaps and of course bounds, the more I drank. "This might not happen in England" I concluded by the morning of the next day. "Ofsted would be involved somewhere".

I spent the whole of March that year in England, intent on going back to Poland early April. This time I had arranged somehow to stay over for three weeks. It was to be an Easter break. Three weeks! That Kylie was so open to collusion. Or perhaps she too knew what it was like to love from afar. Course she did – hadn't Donovan worn his multi-coloured sweatshirt up Soho way some years before? Poor Kylie. She could never get front row tickets and she knew that love could hurt so.

That April visit would prove to be powerfully emotional for me for one reason alone. And although nothing it seemed could now separate us, neither time, space or Stock Aitken and Waterman, something did come very close. Something I never expected could or would happen. Another part of my life was about to change forever.

CHAPTER EIGHT

DIES IRAE

Around the beginning of April 2006 I took myself off to Poland once more. My first Polish Easter. I had left behind a family not entirely convinced of my decision to travel on this occasion. It was the middle of the month whilst waiting for Marta to finish work that I found myself sitting quite graciously in the fine little drinking den 'John Bull.' The sun was shining and the city was alive with people going about their daily business. The flower sellers, the arts and craft stalls, the paper couriers hanging on every street corner plying their typical tabloid wares. Life was encapsulated with energy. The taxis lined the kerbs, the birds swarmed and flitted between the imposing buildings so vibrant in colour. The gushing fountain in the centre of the square sprayed water in a springtime whisper. Life had been re-invented, unlocked from a cold harsh winter. Apt then of course that it was Easter where rebirth or new life goes by association. Wrocław Rynek, the town square, breathed life and pumped blood through its winding streets and alleys.

'John Bull' is a traditional English boozer. As mentioned before, pictures of British battles long since forgotten adorn the walls and are accompanied, I discovered on this occasion, by a large brass gramophone I had not seen before, and an over-played piano in the corner. The carpet is patterned and well-trodden. A television hangs between two large screens on a bracket in one corner where sport is watched of an evening. Hoards of expats invade this establishment as you might expect. It is a genuine home from home. The smell is of Old Blighty too. The tables, the chairs, the wallpaper seem to give off a scent which only a traditional English pub can manufacture. It permeates around you as soon as you walk in. A chemical admixture of Guinness, English breakfasts, a bag of nuts and perhaps a few pork scratchings. All resting in her Majesty's honour atop the furniture-polished bar and the brasso-rubbed copper and zinc alloy.

I was drinking Tyskie. A smooth lager extremely popular with the Poles and increasingly so with the English. Available I now believe, in Wetherspoons. I had at that point just arrived back from Góra, the home of course of Marta's parents, some 60 kilometres away in the rural heartlands of Poland, having just experienced an Easter, much like Christmas, steeped in religion and tradition. On the day before Easter Day we had to paint eggs using a variety of colours and fill a small basket with a myriad of different ingredients like bread, ham and salt. A small pot of horseradish sauce and boiled eggs made up this crucifixion menu. The following day members of the family would dress up nicely and walk down to church or in our case the nearest road-side cross. Poland is awash with these saintly wooden monoliths. Huge in stature – often some twenty feet high and decorated with flowers and candles at the bottom they add some colour to the otherwise gloomy road you may be travelling down. The praying masses flock to these religious outposts in their dozens. A priest invariably turns up late and starts to conduct a service as best he can to the cacophony of cars, lorries and the occasional drunk on a bike not feet from his neatly ironed priest-whites, which flap gently to and fro as each heavy vehicle passes by.

Our beautiful little basket was blessed as were all the others by the priest with Holy water, which involved dipping an object that looked like the Olympic flame into a pot of liquid and dousing the baskets and the standing congregation with Jesus H20.

After this tradition, once back at home, the family tucked into a veritable feast including all the dishes of which the basket ingredients were a part of. The food does not seem to end. And didn't end that Easter day.

But despite all this there was another more humble aspect to this particular Easter. Marta's nan had been taken ill and the doctors were not entirely sure whether she would pull through. Her nan at that time was around 85 years old. We spent several days in hospital sitting at her bedside. Whether it was fate or perhaps Marta's mum's home-cooked food in glass jars, she did however, much to our collected delight and relief, pull through. But no sooner had the old dame been given the all-clear than I received a phone call from England from my mother. My Nan had also been taken ill and had taken a turn for the worse given her ongoing treatment for cancer. I took a call from my mother, Barbara, and asked whether I should come home, my return journey being a week hence. Mum said that I may as well stay out in Poland for now and that she would let me know if the situation changed.

I didn't really know what to do. I could have jumped on the next plane home and have been with Nan for what might have been her last moments, or I could have stayed in Poland and kept the faith that for one more week she would hold on. I opted to stay. Over the next few days we went to the church in Góra and I sat with eyes transfixed on a huge painting of Jesus pre-cross which was hung above the altar. I don't remember whether I actually prayed to Him in the true sense of the word – my faith is more abstract than religiously aligned – but I found myself asking questions in a way that I had never done before. "Why?" being perhaps the operative one.

I thought about Fareham a lot. I thought about Red Triangle Marta and whether I should return and try to block out everything with a few more smoky evenings on the staff house sofa. She had been having a few problems at work at this point as I recall and had expressed an interest in going back to Poland. She had become snappy, depressed and not very approachable. Certainly her views or opinions had become more extreme and were reflected in her twists in sobriety. Suddenly a huge gulf had opened up between us. I was in love with a beautiful woman in Poland, her own country, and she had begun to hate life in the country I may have called my own. She started to see me as an intrusion I believe and would often shut herself away from everyone. I would be a conceited fool to say she became envious of what I had. Others might not. And others did not. I concluded that her time in the UK was coming to an end and that maybe it was time to move on. For her. Either way I kept my distance from then on. I remember telling her about my Nan and will forever remember her response.

"I'm just waiting for my nan to die so that I can move into her house in Poland."

I saw her true colours that night. Or maybe that was what she had come to. We all had issues but she had gone a step further in her barbarity.

English life corrupts, but absolute English life corrupts absolutely.

Monday the 24th of April was my last full day in Poland. I was to catch the 6pm bus back to London the following evening. I started packing my bits together around morning time and secured for myself a breakfast. I pottered around a bit before getting some stuff together and walking out of the flat in Wrocław and into the bright sunny day. It appeared a day just like any other. I had a job interview to attend as it happened and plonked myself down in a town square bar and ordered a coffee. It was around twelve o'clock. Noon. I drained my coffee and walked the short distance across the square to the imposing building where the school director was waiting to receive me. I did well in that interview. I gained valuable experience again and was able to conduct myself professionally. The director said she would let me know.

Later that same day I went to meet Marta from Hotel Pope and noticed that she was approaching me in a most unorthodox fashion. "What's wrong?" I asked. Marta then proceeded to tell me that my mum had sent a text message to her phone at 1pm that day, to tell her and me that my Nan had died. (I believe we used to correspond this way as Marta's tariff was cheap whereas mine wasn't).

I couldn't take in what she had just said. I stumbled into the kerb and into nearby cathedral walls almost drunkenly. I couldn't speak. For a minute. I felt bereft of laughter, devoid of feeling, of anything. Marta consoled me as best she could and we trudged grudgingly and with broken hearts back to our flat.

Later that evening Marta and I went out to meet a friend. A previously arranged rendezvous in a local bar. I drank. Like a fool. In a stupid attempt to obliterate what had happened that day and in a forlorn cry for help. Nothing felt real that evening. I was drinking as I might've done normally yet something was wrong. It was like I was seeing myself from the outside of my body, or from above. On the periphery of reality I couldn't take it in. I was two people somehow conjoined in tragedy. Separate yet not distinct.

The following evening I travelled back to England. Mum informed me that the funeral would be in a week or so and so we started to plan for something I thought would never come.

PART TWO

EZ/VII/VI

The days leading up to the funeral were mundane and nothing made any sense to me. I couldn't work with any conviction and had the added strain of being apart from Marta. Life was vexing and irking me continually. Everything wore a cloak of black and I seemed to fit it perfectly. Two weeks passed.

Then the day finally arrived and my parents and I (other family members were due to arrive the next day) made our way up to Bexleyheath and into the arms of Granddad who looked solemn and deeply moved. Tears apparent in his eyes. I wondered what I could say to compensate for such a loss. He in my mind and to everyone else was inconsolable.

Gradually though, once the bags had been unpacked and the formalities exchanged, things slowly grew more bearable. Cups of tea were made and some food laid out on the table. Granddad then, I have no idea how, astonished me by talking about his neighbours, his garden, the 'blasted pigeons' and how difficult he was finding the latest sudoku puzzle! I had been anxious on entering his house over the fact that I had been in Poland when Nan had died but Granddad soon showed me I had nothing to worry about. He was talking like Granddad but was so obviously in bits.

After a quick bite to eat in the lounge we got ready for the viewing. Granddad showed my mum a poem that he wanted to place in the coffin. He was crying in the kitchen. Everywhere was Nan. It was as if she was still there. Her clothes, her cups, her flowers. All that was Nan sat neatly as it had done for years. Her books still stacked as she had left them read or unread, her sweets still in the jar on the table. My postcards from Wrocław pinned up on the dresser in the lounge.

Outside in the hallway though were sympathy cards atop the bureau. Cards that brought home the reality. And her chair. That was the most telling thing. Her chair was empty. I couldn't hear her voice, no singing, no laughter, nothing. The black cloak wore tighter still.

Outside the small chapel of rest in Devonshire Road we congregated and made for the entrance. Small steps. We were greeted by a robust-looking woman, rather stout in appearance and middle-aged. She looked stern. She ushered us into what I presume was a waiting-room of sorts and there we were left for five minutes or so. Then the stout stern-looking lady came back and told us we could go in. Granddad, my mum and dad. And me. We entered a small holding room and shuffled forward towards an even smaller room containing the coffin of Nan. We all peered in unison. Nan looked asleep. She was covered by a delicate white blanket and a veil leaving only her face visible. Her eyes shut tightly as if in silent contemplation. In the seconds it took for me to take in all of this I suddenly lost all control of my emotions and sobbed and sobbed and sobbed. My mum read out a prayer and tucked a small card into the coffin from my brother, Keith, which read :

"To Nan, I know I always beat you at 'Spot the Dog' but you will always be a winner to me."

This referred to a memory game my brother always used to play with Nan and which he invariably always won.

We stayed in that small room for about a quarter of an hour with Granddad the last to leave. As I turned to leave myself I uttered a final goodbye and a goodbye in Polish from Marta too.

"Żegnaj babciu, spoczywaj w pokoju. Bóg z tobą."

The funeral itself went well. As more family arrived we drove down to the cemetery in Blackfen, near Bexleyheath. Everyone wore suits and looked groomed to perfection. I remember that afternoon Granddad cutting his fingernails. He had to look the part. Nan would have been proud of him. We followed the black hearses into the grounds and past the chapel. As we drove slowly along the streets I noticed some Pakistani builders stop working, and further down the road an elderly gentleman walking his dog bowed his head. Nan would have respect.

The service was conducted by an elderly priest who seemed to know of Nan and Granddad personally and who wore a genuine expression of grief. He related various tales of how Nan used to badger Granddad to remove insects from the house without killing them, or which radio station they liked to listen to in bed. Personal anecdotes but told with compassion. The rows of onlookers began weeping at this stage with Granddad leading the tearful crescendo. And then came the end. We all glanced at the coffin sat on a table behind the priest, adorned with blooms and bouquets and dozens of prayers as it slowly began to slide behind the curtain to a sombre dirge of tune and tears.

Outside the flowers kept coming. Well-wishers and family became one large group of condolence. Granddad's card perched beside a large bunch of colourful red roses with the words:

"To my darling wife Kathleen – thank you for being in my life for 63 years. Goodnight and God bless."

Back at what was now just Granddad's house. A little after 3pm. Melancholy grew without respite. The food laid out on the table offered little in the way of remedy. There were snippets of conversation that threatened to blossom into something more alluring but I could not shake off that black cloak. Yet I tried to be strong for Granddad. At one point I was in the front room explaining the cultural and political differences of Poland to various relatives from near and afar! Nan must have been proud of me. But to me the subject was banal and I felt pangs of guilt talking about how my life was exemplary over in Poland when my Granddad's was broken.

As the afternoon turned into the evening people shuffled away in their ones and twos until only the core relatives were left. Mum, dad, my brother, sister, two cousins and their parents. We sat with Granddad and cried once again.

When I left that evening with my parents and siblings, and saw Granddad slowly walk back inside his house where for 63 years Nan, his beloved wife had lived, I had such a sense of desolation and mundanity about life itself that I did not know how to compose myself. I thought I would have to listen to that funeral dirge in my head forever.

Yet it was not so.

A few days later towards the middle of May 2006 I had a phone interview. I had received an email from a school in Wrocław asking me if I would be available to receive a call to discuss possible employment in the city from September. One of the schools I had visited with Marta a month before had responded and if successful on the old blower I was to meet the director to discuss terms!

A nightmare spent in the mire so black, was life about to ebb and flow again? A volcanic eruption of fate spewing distinction and separation with opportunity and chance. The alchemy of life itself.

CHAPTER NINE

ORA ET LABORA

That phone interview went well. I telephoned a long-winded number and spoke with initial trepidation to a seductively-voiced lady from Poland, and despite my brain telling me several times that here was an opportunity to speak dirty, I conducted myself in a proper manner, although never have verbs, nouns and conditional clauses been spoken with so much unrequited eroticism.

I was to wait but a little time until the school made a decision and in fact in the end it wanted just a couple of weeks. Marta had joined me in England towards the end of May and I, in my excitement, had travelled up to meet her off the coach from Wrocław at Victoria, London. After meeting up and exchanging the news we sat down to use the internet at a cafe just off of the station itself, and I opened up my account. I had begun to despair of getting a reply to be honest. One week had gone by and I had started to resign myself to the fact that on this occasion I might not have struck gold. But I wasn't too despondent for I had other options and a few other avenues I wished to explore. There were many schools in Wrocław and over the last few months I had visited a good number of them with my CV tucked under my arm and a beautifully constructed covering letter complete with non-criminal looking photo in the top-right hand corner. I was nothing if not professional.

Marta ordered a coffee from the adjacent Burger King outlet and we watched as my account opened for all to see. I was like Charlie Bucket perched on his flea-ridden grandparents' bed (coach station plastic chairs are notoriously spasmodic) slowly unwrapping a Wonka bar. A glimmer of what? A flash of something?

What did my eyes alight upon on that electronically-written page?

"*Dear Gary*

Thank you for your recent application and the phone interview conducted by Mrs Seductive-Sounding Polish Lady.

We would like to offer you the job of English Language Teacher effective from September 11th 2006. Please find attached all relevant information regarding this offer.

Please confirm whether you wish to take up this opportunity by email to reach us not later than May 31st.

May I thank you once again for the interest you have shown in our school and we look forward to meeting you in due course.

Yours Kindly

Somebody who was probably Director of Studies."

Marta nearly spilled her coffee as we looked at each other in astonishment. I had done it! I had secured employment in another country! My Golden Ticket!

I would soon be meeting up with Mike TV, Veruca Salt and Augustus Gloop to boot.

Here was a thing. After the initial euphoria had evaporated a little we were left with the realisation that things were about to change for us and alternative realities were about to become science-fact not fiction again. I needed Emmett Brown to explain all this. I couldn't take it in straight away. I had so many questions to ask. "Am I up for the challenge? What clothes did I need to buy? Where would we live? How was I going to tell my parents? What the devil is a phrasal-verb?" We bought another coffee to avert a panic attack and because Marta's was mostly seeping into the keys of the keyboard and/or dripping off the desk and onto the sticky floor below.

I recalled that old maxim again. Post nubila, Phoebus. Was it finally working the right way at last? I emailed my acceptance.

Over the next few weeks I started to study the course materials I had been supplied with and began visiting the library as often as I could. I wanted to learn as much as I could over the summer before I made my move. I was to have two weeks off-site training to wean me into the job but I wanted to go over with at least some idea of what they wanted me to do. I was nervous. Like that first flight I took in 2005. Like my last visit to the dentist. Yet this was a whole new and different animal.

The world cup started that summer. I tried my best to follow it as much as I could which obviously meant for a few matches, but when we lost again on penalties to Portugal this time my interest waned.

It was on one of these afternoons that I met up with an old friend. A lovely girl called Melissa. We had fallen out a few years before over something trivial no doubt. I think I decided not to like her latest squeeze since I myself liked her somewhat. But hadn't realised it till she found another suitor. That old chestnut. My inner jealousy monster aroused its ugly head and took umbrage. But on this particular day we put all those differences of opinion behind us and just enjoyed the game as two mates should. I also think she was single once again so it was even more agreeable. I don't really like it when past-girlfriends or love-interests find other paramours. It always feels like a slight on my person. I don't know why. I should be happy for them. But all that goes through my vague mind is how much better they could have done had they stuck with me.

To this day Melissa and I have continued to let our friendship flourish, though I don't see her as much now as I used to. She is married now to a lovely bloke from Scotland but that in itself is another story and must remain so for the time being. I see that world cup meeting as the day we started speaking to each other again and despite the poor quality finishing by the England strikers on that day, at least I had put something in the back of the net where she was concerned. We stayed friends and over the following few years she would spend many holidays out in Poland having met Marta, and we all became close because of this.

Going into August I found a course that I was quite interested in in London. A teaching course run by a lady whose name I forget now. But this was in The Royal College in The Regent's Park just behind Baker Street. Sherlock's Home. It would lead to a qualification in English Teaching albeit a minor one. In effect it was a crash course which was due to start on the 25th of that month and finish on the 27th. I assumed one weekend was all that was required to teach one how to teach English in its entirety!

That Friday the 25th I took train to London, armed with books, paper, and all things stationery. Thinking back to my passport acquisition nearly two years before, I chose wisely and opted to stay with Donkey who lived at this point in Greenwich. I could've travelled, commuted or stayed at a hotel. All expenses were covered but I embraced masochism. Donkey showed me round his Greenwich flat which was vast by all accounts and I wondered how he could afford such a place but refrained of course from posing such a question unto him. He was doing alright for himself. He had left Fareham some years ago and was odd-jobbing around the city and building up his portfolio as an actor. He had attended Rose Bruford School of Drama in the mid to late nineties and had been knocking on the door since with some degree of success. It would be trivial of me to relate all his tales of televisual greatness here but he has, and he won't mind me telling the avid reader this, had bit-parts, or starred I should say in both Eastenders and Crimewatch! Both I have always thought, off-shoots of each other.

We went out for something to eat on the day I unpacked my weekend bag at this great theatrical domain of his. But food as you may expect figured little more that night. We felt it fitting, given the circumstances, that numerous beers were swallowed in earnest. A double celebration. Me about to leave for a new job abroad and him having just been 'jobbing' that day dressed as a ravenous canine advertising Pal dog food outside Asda. It was tough for him at that point before Eastwatch and Crime-enders came a-calling. We must've got back way past midnight and I knew somewhere in the dark recesses of my drink-embalmed mind that I needed to get up quite early. I thought of Marta in Wrocław tucked up snugly in bed.

"I have to do this for her" called out my inner sense of reason which I have constantly relied upon throughout my life. It doesn't matter what I do, what scrapes I get myself into, what troubles or indecisions I come up against, there is always my little guardian-imp-angel that surfaces when called upon or not as the case sometimes is. He guides me back onto the right path and scalds me the way your nan might scald you for eating too many sweets before tea. Without menace or judgement yet somehow oddly forceful.

I jumped on the 8.45am DLR the next morning with spring and fervour. I had missed the 8am one.

I didn't really know what I was about to let myself in for. "The Royal College in The Regent's Park? Sounds awfully serious to me," I thought. And that was what it became. From the moment I turned up late and half-drunk to the time I gained my certificate on the Sunday afternoon, I was a state. The tutor, a lovely middle-aged woman, must've thought I was taking the 'Michael' such was the level of my educational compatriots. They had obviously been here before and had knowledge of grammar and lesson plans and standing up in class in front of two dozen eager students and a few indifferent ones. Either way I had to perform. I had to put on a show. To act. And Donkey was nowhere to be seen. The only part of that course I felt remotely at ease with was when the class reconvened after lunch on the second day and the tutor conducted the next hour in Turkish! To give us some idea of what it felt like to be a foreign student learning English for the first time. Then, to my relief and amusement, we were all on the same level. Blank-looking and moronic. I passed that course though. I have no idea how since I knew nothing and the concepts were alien to me. I kept thinking about

Marta and how proud she would be of me and how this would be the opening to a greater world. She was my motivation in a place I believed I had no right to be. And I suppose, because of these lingering doubts, after this course I had started to think that teaching might not be for me after all, and as I made my weary way back to the tube station giving Holmes a look of disdain, I panicked. There he was all statuesque and smug, sitting on his plinth surveying every inch of Baker Street.

I had already handed in my notice at work and was due to work my last day in about a week. "Had I been too hasty?" The thought echoed in my brain like a yodeller with ADHD. Baker Street was awash with commuters going home from work. People moved quickly through the crowds stopping only to buy an Evening Standard or pick up a bagel. The smell of the fresh bagels inter-twined with the rush of the traffic and seemed to follow me down the escalator and into the bleakness below. I now smelt metallic dirty air and I had to breathe it in. I wished I had bought a bagel.

Back in Fareham out came the guardian-imp-angel again and a sense of reason and rationality. "You have come this far. Don't give up now. You passed the course. Maybe they liked me?" I had about a week to pack my stuff and inform all the relevant bodies of my imminent departure. Banks, post office, utility companies, tax office (I might've been lax here) etc. Marta waited with nervous apprehension. Over the summer she and Magda, the girl she shared the flat with along with the other three students, had found another flat just for the two of them. So it became easier to sort of live a 'normal.' life. Certainly more comfortable and less chance of getting caught with an unwanted and embarrassing erection first thing in the morning or last thing at night what with 5 sets of bras and negligees flying around all over the place. Let it remain a fantasy as in truth of course, the reality was not all that.

By Monday 4th of September my humble flat at the staff house was slowly becoming vacant. I was to move out on Wednesday. My modus operandi was to travel to London to see Granddad in the evening, stay overnight with him and travel to Victoria the next morning. The farewells had been completed by this time and the tears had been wiped away. I was doing it. This great move. This monumental change, this seismic shift.

That same evening just before 8pm, having alighted at Waterloo station, I met Donkey again in a small side-street pub for what proved to be our last beer in England for some years. Resolute and steadfast in my ambition, I did not need to summon the guardian-imp-angel and she remained deep within my soul, alone, probably watching television and munching on a bar of chocolate like a loser. I would not need her services tonight. I was resolved, and as my tenure in the UK crawled to its irreversible conclusion, I silently bid my English life goodbye. Granddad tearfully saw me off in a taxi the next morning and I turned my attention to Poland once more. I had spent the night tossing and turning, much more than usual, and this had resulted in me feeling a knot of tension in the pit of my stomach that would not abate. As I said goodbye to him after breakfast we hugged a farewell hug that did all to span two generations. Bexleyheath train station was my next port of call. And from there to Victoria to catch the Wrocław coach. My journey was in its infancy.

CHAPTER TEN

TEMPUS OMNIA REVELAT

Here there began a period of about a week whereby I was whipped up into a state of frenzy. I perhaps knew that if forced to, I could teach, although I had some reservations. There was, as some folk would often say, as if to give my self-confidence a perk, a latent syntactic talent lurking awkwardly within my soul. But, alas I couldn't seem to access it at the best of times or indeed at the worst of times. Dickens would have been proud. I felt like Philip Larkin14. Everybody would agree I was ready for a new challenge and that I might even begin to excel in it. Yet at the back of my cupboard there dwelt something irksome. Like Larkin's secret pornography stash. He may have been a great author, a gentleman and scholar no doubt, but when you stripped it all down he was just like the rest of us. A grubby little mite with a penchant for a bit of spanking.

I kept telling myself I could teach. I could transfer some of my knowledge of the English language to others in need of the same. Yet despite my constant prayers it remained something that simply could not be imagined. Like the Queen dying, a 'real' moon landing, or your mum getting pregnant again.

As I sat alone in a Polish flat in a city called Gliwice near to the south of the country I contemplated my life. It was 10th of September and Marta had just left me at the train station having accompanied me to this place all starry-eyed and full of expectation. Inside this small place I found all that I could have wished for and on first impressions it looked alright. It was a one-bedroomed accommodation and had a quaint bathroom, a comfortable lounge and a dining area and looked out towards the municipality that was Gliwice. I sat on the sofa and lurched wistfully to the left. The springs were broken. Later I tried to put on the television. It didn't work. When I subsequently discovered that there was no hot water I swore. In English, so as not to cause too much alarm. It was in this fit of frustration that I thumped my fist down hard upon the top of the television which as if by magic, delivered up channel four. In Polish of course. I remembered my father's wise words, "son," he said, "when in doubt, give it a clout." These words have stood me in remarkable stead over the years. I made myself some lunch and sat down. On the chair this time which was made of wood and sturdy-looking. Although I could see a city gurgling with life through the window I felt solitary and isolated. Though at least I was myself which was what I believe all men are when they feel truly alone. I began to make plans for the next day. The day when would begin my new career. Armed with books and papers I started. And so it went on into the evening. I revised as much as I could. I changed my way of thinking. My world view altered to fit this new reality. And after a few cups of tea and several uppercuts to the television I retired to bed. Content was I that I had done all that I could to prepare myself for the days ahead.

As I slept that night I imagined or dreamed of all the possibilities that may open up for me now and all the avenues we as a couple, Marta and I, might now saunter along. But still questions remained. "Could I succeed?" It was impossible to answer. Like so many other posers that tease and vex me constantly through life.

"Where is JD Salinger?

Why do mosquitoes exist?

Did Lee Harvey Oswald really shoot Kennedy?

36

Why is Lebara so bloody expensive compared to O2?

How can rich people successfully avoid paying tax?

Is Lady Gaga a man?

Should you always tip a taxi driver even if they refer to you as a cunt?

Is Gary Glitter wholly bad?"

I was like a sponge soaking up answers and collecting information yet still I wanted more. My head began to feel dizzy. I remembered Patrick McGoohan. Number six. "Questions are a burden and answers a prison to oneself." But I was a free man. Portmeirion is a weird place you know. It might resemble the country of Lilliput as you traipse through its environs with all your western pomp and your yahoo excesses. For I went there once I tell thee. And I felt exactly like this, if at first a little taken aback at the Brobdingnagian entrance fee.

Oh how I love thee Swift. His words. His satire. His erudition. His is a hubristic world derived from the Latin for 'eighteen inches.'

Sesquipedalis. Itself, describing such a length would be a little sesquipedalian. It is what it is. Horace15, the Roman poet, tells us in 'Ars poetica' about the use of long words terming them as sesquipedalia verba. Swift was a proud man I'm sure, for he was a certain sesquipedalianist. Who else could spell or indeed pronounce Hounhynmns? His writing sometimes comes across as sesquipedalianism, though he may not have always stooped to sesquipedality as for it to become habit-forming. Perhaps after all we have pondered here, Swift was just a clever author who liked a bit of nonsense now and again. As we all do. On reflection I do not think of him as an out-and-out hyperpolysyllabicsesquipedalianist.

Education teaches. I was aware in 2006 that I needed to reach a level of presumed education and fast. My C in English Language and Literature was not going to be good enough. I needed something to talk about. I had a thirst for knowledge. A quest. Yet I was only me. However clever or wise, educated even I thought I was, I was still just me. A normal guy who had wandered through life without much direction, occasionally getting lost, sometimes getting lucky with women, falling asleep on midnight trains and abusing television sets. Like Mike Myers in Wayne's World 2 when he meets and tries to chat up Drew Barrymore's character in that office scene. He impresses her with his knowledge of her home country which in the movie happened to be Norway, but then spoils it by telling her that he once got diarrhoea on a trampoline. If I could tell a story like this then maybe I would be on my way to some kind of success. I needed words and phrases and data. And a way to compile everything. Something special. A little different maybe. My own style. Ernest Vincent Wright wrote, in 1939, a novel called 'Gadsby' which consisted of more than 50,000 words and which did not once contain the letter E. "Surely I could do this" I mused.

"A bit similar to that film Wayn's World 2 in which said protagonist wants to chat up Dru Barrymor's girl part in that room. Dru looks as though Wayn is winning with his facts and his words about Norway. But shortly this poor girl is sad and glum as Wayn spoils it by talking about his unlucky day on a jumping mat with springs, upon which a nasty bout of bottom runs did occur."

There. Nothing to it.

I awoke the next morning a pack of nerves yet ready to go. I ambled after breakfast, put my school clothes on and smacked the television. Upon my arrival at the training school which as it happened was also the Head Office of the schools located in Poland in which I was to work, I found my way up to the room where the course was to be run. As I unpacked my meagre possessions I looked around me at the other people who began milling around the room. I then proceeded to meet an American girl, two Australians, husband and wife, a guy from Newcastle, David, who couldn't stop talking about random trivia and of how much he was in debt, and a 6 foot 4 inch bloke from Liverpool called Daniel. This Daniel I initially had reservations about as he was the spitting image of the French lad we used to live with back at the staff house in England. Fareham. How far away I was from its being. Yet here was the dull, insolent guy from Calais, not playing chess or smelling slightly of onions, still less making unwanted advances in any direction, prancing up and down a teacher training school room in Gliwice, southern Poland. Speaking Liverpudlian. Once we got into it the whole experience was undertaken in a somewhat laid-back approach. We as a class started presenting ourselves and learning the stuff by rote straight off. We were given a book and expected to read from it. "Tis easy" I thought. And to an extent so it proved to be. My job, I learnt, was mainly to read to students from a front-facing lectern, from a large blue book. Simple stuff. "What am I doing? Where is the pencil? What is the capital of Spain?" (It got harder the more the student progressed obviously). The learner would learn the questions and then just repeat back an already-written answer from his or her own book. It was simple question-answer with not much room for teacher expressionism. But I found my way around this eventually.

The training course went on for about 10 days and during that time I really got myself into it and started using some of my new-found wit and diarrhoea-based trampoline intelligence. By the end of the time there I was ready to apply myself in a real classroom with real students. My contract at the school required me to move back up to Wrocław which was of course my preferred destination since Marta was living there at the time. And I of course loved her so. So after the course finished and I had collected all my bits and bobs for the new school where I was to begin the actual job, I took train to the city of dreams.

My first class I remember well. It was a class of young girls, all about 17 or 18. Rowdy types. Hormonal perhaps. On maybe. I stood in the middle of this room with the girls in front of me forming a semi-circle of raging sexuality. Luckily I was wearing loose trousers that day and they were at a lower level of English which didn't require me to explain the meaning of anything that might have been connected to Sid James. It went well that lesson. And they did go well from there really. I adapted to it. I grew into it. As I picked up more and more of the grammar so they put me in with higher groups and I would go in armed with confidence. I took it seriously for I wanted to do well, but I also had a lot of fun. Part of the job was to run a monthly club out of school. I would run 'Rock Club' as I quite liked rock music and that was my forte, whereby I mean I had an interest in that genre. I would run rock quizzes and have talks on the big names in the business. I got to take students out to local gigs, all paid for by the school. It was great. "I am living a dream here" I told myself often. There were what you might call 'groupies' who were all over the native English speakers simply because they saw it as a free opportunity to learn the language. Some teachers took advantage of this, but I stayed true to the girl I had laid my life down for. It would have been so easy to have shagged my way around Wrocław from that point but I didn't.

In November I took my little 'devil group' to a local club called 'WZ.' It was a kind of underground alternative scene sort of thing. Everyone wore black, even the bouncers were goths. Marta became almost like my tour manager helping me plan tickets and all. We went to watch the band called 'Closterkeller.' She liked this band and had been following them for a good few years before I had met her. I quickly came to realise that if I drank out of school with students and indulged in all the parties that presented themselves in connection with work, then a more popular teacher I seemed to become. And over the course of the next few months that was indeed what did occur.

And the more successful I became the more Marta would look upon me as her man. I no longer had to pursue her quite so melodramatically. She melted into my hands. No more the gentle persuasion, the stolen kiss on the Warsaw train, the bashful Keppels Head groin strain. I could now command some jiggy-jiggy. Berlusconi's bunga-bunga. I would no more be the chasing Touchstone on the heels of but never quite catching that elusive Audrey. And that was as I liked it. I would say my wooing was more effectual than Touchstone's. For if you think about it isn't that what we all strive for? To love and be loved? Shakespeare knew this – he wrote about it often enough. We are addicted to Bardolatry. But why? Human nature wants to love. We are all desperately seeking that Audrey. Or in Madonna's case, Susan. But do we always find her? Therein lies the conundrum. It must not always be so for we do not live in a utopian world of unicorns and rainbows and multi-coloured ice-pops. That's a fictional world. It can only exist figuratively. In our imperfective imaginations. Unless of course you watch The Magic Roundabout or live in a staff house with a greying old sofa and smoke strange substances all the time. The story of life is simple yet infinitely and morosely depressing. Man hunts woman. Man loses woman. Man then hunts whale. All the stories you have ever read and all of life is just a mixed-up combination of these three ideas. There is nothing else. I wanted to be loved and that was why I gave up my life in sunny old Fareham, complete with its quaint country pubs and its town centre bandstand, and started my search – my chasing. My Audrey.

The title of this particular chapter 'Tempus Omnia Revelat' is perhaps significant in that it was at this point I discovered something more about myself. It took time but I came to see myself as a deeper, more spiritualised human being. I accepted a different culture and all that went with that. I rose up and showed to the world my newly discovered identity.

Towards the end of November of that year I spoke to Marta and we decided to plan for Christmas. A trip back to the Motherland to see everybody after three months of toil in a foreign land. My flag waving gloriously abroad and nobody in England to see it. I had stories to tell and I wanted to tell them.

Magda had a birthday on the 28th and we had a bit of a party for her at the flat in Wrocław and then took her to a local club to see a band called 'Chainsaw.' "Sounds divine" quoth she. The club was called 'Madness' and it was. The lead singer of this band was none other than Paul Di'anno the original singer/vocalist in Iron Maiden. I had not known this as Marta had kept it a secret from me right up until the actual evening. Twas a lovely surprise. It was a classic evening and Paul played all the hits he wrote when in Maiden. 'Phantom of the Opera' was of course the highlight as it always must be. After the show we all got chatting to him and he signed a CD and a tee-shirt for me shortly before hoofing into the toilets to be violently sick. Or that is what he said anyway. He didn't appear to be sober. Straight after the show we took Magda home as she couldn't actually hear anymore and would require the services of a hearing doctor quite soon I ventured. It was around this time that she actually met a lovely guy called Robert. A Polish guy from a town called Krotoszyn who taught young tennis players to play tennis. A tennis trainer by all accounts. Once Magda had regained her hearing after our little Madness he started his own variation on the Man hunts Woman storyline and subsequently won his particular Audrey. Robert couldn't speak too much English so he became like a student to me. I would teach him sentences, useful to him as I thought, and he would buy me the odd beer in town now and again. I picked up several other part-time or private students out of school, which the school directors didn't really look too kindly on but couldn't do much about, since it was not stipulated that we couldn't have extra-curricular activities in the shape of 'privates' as they were known. I had a lovely girl, 18 I think she was, called Karina. She was studying to become a nun! She lived in what you might call a nunnery and there were all these 'women of the cloth' running around during our lessons like Sister Act on acid. I taught her for a few months and she became quite a friend to me and Marta and was a regular source of income. She eventually gave up the lessons as she got so tied up with all the nun stuff and she had to take a lot of exams. Perhaps today she is indeed Sister Karina.

I bought our tickets back to England at the beginning of December and we started to plan what we would do during the two weeks off. My love for Marta grew stronger one misty evening in Wrocław whilst we were eating a pizza at an underground bar. I presented her the tickets in a ribbon and in an envelope whilst we chewed on a Hawaiian and supped Polish beer. She looked into my eyes and smiled and it warmed my heart no end. And despite this pizza joint having a code to get into the toilets it did as I recall smell inexplicably of urine. Something which took the edge off the romance somewhat. Nonetheless I was happy. I had achieved something over those final few months of that year. A phoenix from the ashes again. I was going places with the one I loved and I realised that I didn't really need to be much of a hyperpolysyllabicsesquipedalianist to get on in teaching. You just needed love. I beamed as we finished our meal that evening and a tear swam down my cheek. "Co sięstało kochanie?" she said endearingly. I smiled and sighed back at her. "Wszystko w porządku, ale naprawę tesknię za mojąbabcią."

And I did so wish she could have seen me then.

CHAPTER ELEVEN

OPUS NEGOTIUM ET LACRIMAS

As the year rolled forward I grew into the job in Wrocław. I can't say I took to it like a duck takes to the water as they say, as there were several parts of the English language, in particular the grammar, that I felt defied interpretation.

I struggled over 'active and passive voice' and winced at 'special verbs' and their infinite uses. But slowly, I suppose bit by bit, I became more adept at presenting my lessons, and this was verified by the Head of Department or Head Teacher during his numerous observations of me 'in situ.'

My relationship with Marta seemed to replicate my improving work situation. We began to go from strength to strength and were not slow in making further decisions that were to affect our immediate future.

We tentatively talked about moving out of the flat we had been living in at that point with Magda, and perhaps 'going it alone.'

Marta began thinking about buying a car. The rationale being that by becoming more mobile, freer maybe, that this would lead to more success. Marta wanted to register me as a 'working citizen' living in Poland and started to ask about what might be done about actual citizenship, and whether or not

40

this would bring advantages. These ideas and various others began buzzing around our heads and became simultaneously more and more alluring and confusing like Hardy's 16 hexagons to the bee.

By the beginning of December 2006 the school had picked up a major new contract just outside Wrocław's city centre. Siemens. A bit of a coup over competing schools in the area.

Siemens in Wrocław was a large company on one of the longest streets in town. Grabiszyńska Street. Don't attempt to walk its length unless you have adequate footwear, GPS and something edible. Enough perhaps to cover a small number of impromptu picnics or breaks that will invariably crop up along its laborious route.

Luckily for me, when I taught there, I took the tram and the school reimbursed me. I don't know why but I seemed to be sent to Siemens quite often. Maybe I showed willing or passed muster or something. I got the impression that the other teachers did not. I wasn't overly bothered to be honest, it was extra money and a chance to benefit from some off-the-job training to improve or enhance my school work. Maybe it was simply that I, in those days, displayed an air of respectability in my corporate attire consisting of smart black shoes, white cotton shirt and a neat haircut. All of this in stark contrast to my colleagues, most of whom offered varying designs of sneaker, expletive-ridden tee-shirts and hair that, in hue, included all the colours of the rainbow. Maybe it was this.

I didn't care. I was proud to be able to go to this firm and hold conversations with these high-fliers who must have been earning a small fortune. And here I learnt something.

It seemed to me that the more money a student had or the more professional he or she was, so the more inclined he or she was to talk rhubarb. I found these people happy to joke around with, fun to laugh with and easy to connect with. Not serious-minded, conservative or stern at all, which was perhaps my initial impression. I suppose they saw me as a release. They spent so much time number-crunching, building whatever it was they built or made, empires maybe, that when I rolled off the bus or tram with my torn books and my tales of intrigue and folly from the Motherland, they saw me as a relief. They let themselves go.

I remember one particular student from around the same time. This guy was the president of this small firm of city bailiffs. His office, as I recall, was awash with artefacts he or perhaps his brutish minions had obviously recovered from various poor souls across town, who unfortunately could no longer afford their loan repayments or whatever financial contracts they might have had.

So, this firm of sharks would then 'pay a visit' to these wretches and purloin whatever took their fancy in lieu of repayment. As a consequence this man-president had an incredible array of bric-a-brac in this office, some inconsequential in value but others hugely financially and perhaps sentimentally significant. There were numerous paintings, lots of sports equipment, jewellery, ornaments and an aquarium complete with all sorts of tropical fish all proudly swimming around without a care in the world (fish have no financial worries or burdens) amongst the piratical hoard.

It was extraordinary. He was like the Sheriff of Nottingham collecting bad debts and taxes from the meek and the defenceless. He had two or three secretaries who worked for him in this office, to whom he would frequently bark orders at.

"Bring in tea, and fast!" he implored.

"And for the teacher?" came a timid response from a young snip of a girl.

"Two teas, now!" soon put her in her place.

I remember once, this poor secretary having placed two teas in front of us in his office, only to be met with this sensational masculine line -

"And biscuits. Get them!"

It may have been that his English was not that great and that he was simply translating in his head from his own language (which can at times seem linguistically direct) into what he thought was acceptable in English. In fact I knew this to be true. But to an extent. His English did struggle to obtain mediocrity, but as I got to know him, and from the forlorn resigned looks on the secretaries' faces, I realised that this was a man for whom chauvinism was distinctly understood. I also felt that if Australian-born feminist and eminent authoress Germaine Greer were ever to show her face about town he would have had her horse-whipped over the border quick smart.

I, despite all this, was always treated like a king in his palace. Of course I was. I had an Adam's apple, a deep(ish) voice and a bouncing pair of virile testicles.

He loved to just chat for the entire duration of the lesson. Not about anything I wanted to talk about or teach but about himself. He would disregard the actual lesson plan and grammar and just talk. As a result, in the two years I taught this man, we never got past page 93 of his English workbook!

And now to return to my earlier analogy. The Siemens Analogy.

He was obviously a rich man. Is there such thing as a poor bailiff? Yet despite this he was intent to fool around with me for 90 minutes, eat digestive cookies, sip Earl Grey and discuss how high cheek-bones, short skirts and ample bosoms typified the average Polish girl. Though here I was in agreement. They do.

Polish girls are a revelation. A breed apart. In a Bill Hicks (controversial American satirist and comedian) kind of drug anecdote, "Not all Polish girls are attractive. Some are stunning." I can also use my own - "Even the ugly girls in Poland, and of course there are some, are moderately handsome."

One of the teachers I taught with was a young Jewish girl from America whose name was Jamie. She had arrived in late October and was waiting patiently for her boyfriend who was not scheduled to get to Poland before March 2007. Subsequently she had a lot of time on her hands and we spent some of that time out and about. She had an inquisitive explorational mind. She liked asking questions and travelling.

One day in early December she bribed me into eating in this Jewish restaurant. "Hey, Gary, I'll buy you a beer if you eat a Jewish meal." I think after the words "I'll buy you a beer" I switched off. Anything could have followed this really and the answer would've remained the same, like Led Zeppelin's musical offering.

"Affirmative Jamie."

"Hey Gary, I'll buy you a beer if you assassinate the Prime Minister."

"Hey Gary, I'll buy you a beer if you perform fellatio on my small Jewish poodle."

If you can read the above lines with an American accent, amusingly it is sexier.

I was slowly learning that there was in this city a kind of entertainment culture whereby beer, vodka, and the like were seen as everyday necessities like your daily grocery shop.

"I'm just popping down the road for a couple of shot glasses and a bottle of Zubrowka. I'll pick up a paper and a pint of milk on the way back."

This way of life began to envelop me slowly at first but with ever-increasing malevolence.

I sat in this restaurant with Jamie, with a Tyskie in front of me, while she tried her best to translate the menu into something I could imagine.

Unsure as I was sat in this small eatery, this den of Jewish intrigue, full of trinkets and clutter of a Jewish nature no doubt, I felt obliged enough for her to show me some of the cuisine. And to be honest it wasn't bad. We ate but I do not know what we ate.

It actually resembled the bailiff's extravagant office we heard tell of earlier, though on a smaller scale. And I presume none of the queer little ornaments was recovered from customers who might not have been able to settle their hefty bill.

"What? You can't pay? OK. We'll have your wedding ring, your wristwatch and the shirt off your back Sir."

And any protestations that said shirt was not bought in a Zionist Marks and Spencer would all be in vain.

And so towards Christmas we hurtled. Wrocław looked so beautiful. So festive. Like a Christmas should look. A Christmas of old steeped in tradition. The whole city started to resemble a scene from Mr Fezziwig's Ball17 in 'A Christmas Carol.' The town square tree was also all a tree should be. A spruce. From Norway. And real. And at about 40 foot tall it put our plastic 36 inch model which sat upon our dressing table at home, to shame.

I thus developed a sentimental approach to Christmas. I was abroad in all this Yuletide decadence feeling all ye olde and about to transfer myself back to Fareham to regale my family with my tales of the last three months of my life, which they had largely been unaware of.

I couldn't wait to return. The excitement built as December wore on. It wasn't a longing to be back in the UK particularly or a yearning for the foibles of it, but simply because I thought three months, nearly four was a long time to be apart from family.

I'd never really been apart from them before. I'd always had them at arm's length. A wealth of advice as they always had been. This was back in the day when Facebook, Skype and all that baloney were mere foetuses. Tadpoles on the verge of frogs. Transmogrification had not yet occurred either technologically or in my ability to outgrow letter-posting or email and grasp the Brave New World which loomed ever larger on the horizon, bobbing slowly on towards the shore-line like some irreversible Huxley-esque18 social media D-Day.

The Charge of the Skype Brigade. You can fire your muskets of Russian disgust and indifference but in the end it will get through. So Alfred Tennyson19 told us.

Honour the noble 600 kilobytes.

To come back to literary normality, it was around this time that Melissa contacted me and promised a festive gathering back in our local pub – The Miners Arms. This English pub suddenly began to take on a somewhat ethereal image in my mind. Natural quick-fire wit and repartee. The dartboard, the beer-stained carpets, the smell of the open fire warming the hearts and the cockles of the cheery punters, cheeks rosy red with western extravagance.

John Bull in Wrocław was close but still a field's length away.

The week before Christmas Jamie invited all the teachers and a few choice students to her flat for a Jewish breakfast, which on reflection seemed a bit Uncle Sam. Croissants, pancakes, orange juice and maple syrup.

Jamie's flat was decorated with photos of her boyfriend whose name, I learnt, was Scott. She was missing him no end it appeared, but with so many tiny Kodak images dotted around her flat he seemed to become flesh. There was even one photo tucked behind the bathroom mirror opposite the toilet, peering out all shyly at all and sundry whilst penny-spending took place. He was a good-looking young chap but it was still unnerving.

Because of this when I did finally meet this guy some three months later I couldn't help feeling a sense of familiarity. Like I already knew him. He'd seen my nether regions and that signalled a degree of proximity in my book.

I was not and indeed am still not, a great flier. Planes are not my favoured mode of transport. I'm nervous throughout the whole experience as previously noted, and anything that might make that experience worse is, in my opinion, a step unto Death. That step now shimmered before me in all its ghostly threat.

In England, across the country, a thick blanket of fog and cloud had descended menacingly like a little imp-child or the girl from The Exorcist slowly coming down after a bout of levitation. It was refusing to disperse. Many flights across the land were being cancelled, leaving passengers delayed or stranded in airport lounges with nothing to do but watch robotic cleaning machines and listen to Russian or Spanish girls playing mundane songs on their collective Walkmen.

Such was the disruption that it made the news, the BBC revelling in the frustration of Britain's unfortunate festive holiday-makers.

44

I've always felt the BBC 'doesn't dislike it' when people suffer or tragedies occur. It seems to me that they over-play things a little. Dramatise distress to an unnecessary point. It excites them. It must do. It pays their wages.

Remember that flood in 1998 in Mozambique? Terrible scenes. People losing their homes and many drowning. Remember the headlines? We all saw the consequences.

Lives ruined: But wait! There's a helicopter aloft! Hovering, filming above rooftops. It catches a man. Desperate and clinging on for his life. The rest of his life submerged.

"Help!" he shouts in anguish.

"Sorry, we can't mate, we're full." comes the reply.

I would wager that of course they were full. There's a whole BBC camera crew, two pilots and six interns along for the experience and to enhance their collective broadcasting CVs, on-board.

It makes news doesn't it? Tragedy. But perhaps there is a better way to report, I don't know. Perhaps a different approach might save lives? I'm just putting something out there.

Take Bob Geldof and his town of Boom-Rats. I recall the scenes in Ethiopia in the eighties. Terrible visions of people, emaciated and starving. Awful scenes played out to us through our TV sets. Yet perhaps we were guilty as we watched those skeletal bodies waste away. The tears of the desert-kids, flies crawling lazily over their near-dead bodies. And their eyes all a cursing as they looked pitifully into the camera. We felt cursed through them. Watching them. Were we, in our virginal western opulence guilty of this? A part of the crime? Did we, in fact, slay the albatross in all our ignorance and culinary grandeur?

In Coleridge's20 'Ancient Mariner' in 1797 he depicted a scene so vivid, so clear, so laced with clarity that a better allegory is here hard to envisage. Picture those poor wraiths crying, starving, pleading into our cameras. Now imagine them fed up, livid and revengeful so that through them we ourselves become entangled within their webs of despair.

"One by one, by the star-dogged moon, too quick for groan or sigh, each turned his head with a ghastly pang, and cursed me with his eye. Four times fifty living men, and I heard nor sign nor groan. With heavy thump, a lifeless lump, they dropped down one by one."

Logic might dictate from this that the Ancient Mariner must in fact be Bob Geldof. He does look a bit nautical if you break it all down. Six degrees of separation from that old sea-faring land-lubber Captain Birdseye. Check it out on Ancestry.Com.

Poor Bob, forever cursed to wander the Earth re-telling his tale to unsuspecting wedding guests – and with the speed at which marriage is falling out of fashion in today's society, his days might be numbered.

And then what? He will become his own painted ship upon his own painted hopeless ocean. No wonder he doesn't agree with Mondays. Each one brings him one step closer to this eternal pictorial Death.

45

Ethiopia was gut-wrenching. Yet we tucked into dinners and loosened our belts as courses flowed into our own desserts. But we gave. Or some of us did. Amid these sickening images, we gave. We fed the world and some of them even knew it was Christmas. For a while.

Yet had Bob and the television broadcasters and newsmen alerted us to an impending crisis a bit earlier, six weeks maybe, who knows, more could've been done. But that is the problem isn't it? That doesn't make headlines does it?

"We fancy a sandwich" say Ethiopians.

Eventually, backtracking somewhat, the fog over the UK did clear away and we packed our cases. Mum called to say that Dad would pick us up from Gatwick and collect us off the Centralwings flight. I felt a little more cultured than when I had left three months before. I had consumed a new life and I was eager to tell of it. I wondered whether I would fall back into all things English. I worried about scrambling for the right word in response to a perfectly trivial question. "Perhaps my developing Polish will remain centre stage" I mused. I wanted not only to once again be Among The Brits but equally of them too.

In reality of course I was worrying about nothing. There were no information gaps. Writing about it now I had everything to look forward to. A festive break back in Fareham with my Granddad, mother, father, brother and sister. How would I react to them all correctly with practicality and with manner? With tact and with reason? My sense and sensibilities21 were heightened, my Marianne and Elinor complexes all entwined. Because there was one person who would not be there that Christmas.

When we got back to England I recall thinking how much Granddad deserved the best time with the family that Christmas. What I had achieved that year I believed, was less important than making sure he enjoyed himself as much as was possible. I did miss my Nan. I wanted to recreate a Fezziwig Ball back in Fareham. For Granddad. Because without Nan, I reflected, Christmas would be an angel short.

CHAPTER TWELVE

FORTITUDINE VINCIMUS

Granddad tried hard to enjoy the festivities with us as a family but I could only guess at what he was truly feeling inside. It was his first Christmas without his wife, his one true love, for nearly three score years and ten. He cried. I think we all did at that time. It was hard not to imagine Nan opening her presents with joy and wonder etched across her face, smiling at her family over a cup of tea and a mince pie.

As it was Christmas 2006 passed in delightful abandon. We all set out to embrace the year-end with what a predictable man might term 'spring and vigour.' On Christmas Eve we all went to midnight mass at our local church in Fareham. It is a sombre church at the best of times as most churches I'm sure must be. Something about this one though is different. The graveyard is in places quite overhung by trees, branches drooping as if to pay their own flora and fauna respects to the sleeping dead below. The stones themselves are moss-ridden and moist with dew no matter the season. The wind blows gently through the trees and the grasses and they sway in unison. A whispered recantation for those so close but no longer present. Every soul buried here seems to have been so for hundreds of years. The recently deceased are conspicuous by their absence. There is nothing to instil a smile within the stone walls which surround this church and its various religious outhouses. It is the Deathly Hallows for all who breathe its air, as Rowling probably would've observed. Inside the church itself the mood does not lift. Great paintings of the Holy man on his morbid path to crucifixion litter the cold stone walls, with adjoining exhibits of angels and Mary Magdalene surrounded by harp-playing nymphs. All have Death in their eyes.

Just a moment's digression here - If you look closely you may wonder as I often have about the size and structure of their respective wings. I'm talking of course about these harp-playing angels all saintly and all. Some of the wings are themselves relative to the size of the angel. But some and one in particular I may mention here, have enormous flying aids. The one in question is the Archangel Gabriel. They look like a rocket propulsion unit. Like something the space shuttle shrugs off when it has achieved altitude enough. The thing I often mused over as a young church-going lad is what it sounded like when one of these angels opened her wings and took off. From the ground I mean. The smaller winged fairies and such like I can imagine don't emit much sound at all. Much like a pigeon or a ring dove might when preparing itself for flight. But what of the Archangel Gabriel? What in God's name must she sound like when getting herself airborne? I have posed this question unto myself for many years without much of an answer from Heaven or on high and I can now perhaps enlighten my reader with something of an epiphany. I am of the opinion that she sounds, on opening her wings, much akin to the sound of someone opening up a large golf umbrella.

Anyway as I was recalling. The Deathly Hallows does not relent, neither inside nor out. The carpet on the long walk down the aisle to the altar is worn and ragged. Where once were intricate coloured designs no doubt, now lay only blurred outlines or smudges beaten in by a thousand different pairs of boots. The pews are dark wood and scratched by an equal number of fingers. An occasional floor tile wobbles loose. The Bibles are also loosely distributed, not everyone has one. The Gideon's must have run out after visiting the Post House up the road.

And thus I, to that morbidity came. With my family and with Marta. Dressed up festively and warmly and with deft nods of our heads we saluted the sleepy congregation. The Christmas hymns were sung in a monotone way and were in no way joyous. Marta and I held hands as 'Hark the Herald Angels Sing' was announced. I looked into her eyes and saw something that I had not seen before. Good intent. Visions of the future. Our future. I moved further into her heart and we seemed to converse without speaking. The priest seemed to be talking to us directly. It was like we were the only ones there. Then all of a sudden and without warning I developed a rather tight knot in the pit of my stomach. I had been eating a lot of nuts that day and had knocked back one or two sherries with my mother. I don't want to dwell on this too much but I kind of knew that an emission would probably follow shortly. Things were suddenly not all bright and beautiful and I wasn't sure about morning, but something had definitely broken. I could not allow this to happen though. Not in church and in front of Marta and my family all unsuspectedly singing. In short I thought on my toes. I slinked off during a quiet part of 'Hark the Herald Angels Sing' and, all unseen, meandered into a side room where all the priests' robes were hung and therein broke an extraordinary amount of wind.

After the service we all met the priest and shook hands with him. My family as part of their gratitude, me, by way of an apology.

Over the next few days we met all our old friends once again. Melissa looked well and we caught up on all the gossip. She was intrigued by my tales of Poland and said that she would try to pop over for a visit early in 2007. Marta wanted to drive up to the hotel to see some of her friends who were still working. Red Triangle Marta was still there and was in fact at work when we popped in. She told us that things were not the same there anymore and were not as fun as they were when we all lived there in the staff house under that one roof. It was clear she wasn't happy at the hotel at this point and sure enough it wouldn't be long before she, too, would trace her way back to Poland.

Marta and I travelled to Portsmouth one day and spent some time shopping. She had by now developed an addiction to the large clothing store, Primark. On this particular occasion she went to town, literally. Happily we had our mobile phones and stayed in touch as after the first hour my attention waned a little. I proposed a little walk outside and decided to trudge down to the Guildhall Square where we had seen Whitesnake two years before. Coverdale was not there though on this day, but Wetherspoons was. Feeling a tiny bit hungry after looking at all the pretty dresses and crop tops I opted to take lunch and keep my phone next to me. I needn't have worried. My lunch break concluded after 90 minutes and two beers and Marta still had not been in touch. I wandered back towards Primark and found to my astonishment that she hadn't moved but 5 metres from the pretty dresses she had been eyeing up some two hours before! Another hour went by and we finally made our way to the tills. Frustratingly without a pretty dress. It was after this mammoth shopping experience that I formed an opinion on Marta that stands to this day. When Primark is mentioned always be prepared with a few pounds in your pocket for lunch and a good book to read. You may not read the whole book of course but you may stand a fair chance of deciphering what the blazes Proust was on about during his 'turning over in bed' narrative. That still riles me.

The weather this Christmas was perhaps predictable. An English Christmas usually throws up the same. It was cold, damp and miserable. But I liked it. It was to me English. Poland I had learnt was simply cold in winter. It could never be damp, still less miserable. That was Poland though. Each had its own barometric identity. Through Marta I was able to see the differences between the two countries. Quaint as they were. It was like she was showing me a new world and I, in all my infantile wonder loved her more and more for it.

To keep with things English though for a bit here. On our flight back to Poland we met a quintessential English man. Mother and Father had dropped us off at Gatwick and we sailed through the airport towards our waiting plane. Twas in the queue for the checked baggage that I caught sight of someone from Wrocław. An English man. His name was Phil. Phil was in his mid-forties, roughly shaven and always wore a scraggy old hat. A bit like that which Geoffrey Boycott of cricket and sexism fame might once have donned. He resembled, in my opinion, a bastard son of rabbit crooners Chas or Dave. Despite this he spoke well. He'd an education it was evident. I had spoken to him numerous times in Wrocław. He was a singer, hence the Chas and Dave analogy, and used to belt out hits of old like 'My Way' by Sinatra, or that rude ukulele hit by George Formby. He would stand outside the various buildings in the square and sing and people would, on occasion, throw him coins or sometimes folding money. This is not as incredible as it may seem when you remember we are dealing in a different currency, somewhat weaker than sterling. Whereas a fiver in the UK might be a rudimentary English breakfast with a cup of lukewarm tea, a fiver in Poland might just about be a box of safety matches. (How can matches be safe? Another teaser that vexes me continually).

48

Phil's prime choice of location was always outside McDonald's. And that is where I often met him and we would speak of times past in good old Blighty like we'd been away from it for decades. Like we were political exiles. Which in truth I think he was. Maybe not political so much but I do remember once he told me that he owed the tax-man several English breakfasts and a large number of boxed safety matches. I'm not going to comment on the quality or otherwise of Phil's singing talents. He is what we in the UK have an abundance of. Watch X-Factor. He yearns after eccentricity and it doesn't make itself hard to get. Marta didn't quite understand this Englishness. To her Phil was just weird and she did all she could, at Gatwick, to divert my attention and steer us in the opposite direction. With regards to our plane journey of course. She didn't think him so weird that she actually steered me out of the airport and back down the M23. Mercifully for Marta, Phil actually sat at the front of the plane when we did board and we nudged our way along and sat on the wing. From then on I just immersed myself in the 'Daily Star' and tried to forget that I was in fact 33,000 feet above land!

We flew without incident of course and met Phil again at passport control where he acknowledged us for the first time. Once through customs and baggage reclaim we hopped on the bus together and travelled back to the city centre regaling each other with our respective Christmas stories. Marta this time immersed herself in her edition of 'Gazeta Wyborcza' and from time to time looked out of the window nonchalantly.

I went back to work on the 29th of December and it started to snow. Wrocław had a few inches and it was cold but to use the aforementioned weather analogy, still without any dampness or misery.

We travelled up to Góra to see Marta's parents and were fed to bursting point as usual. Then on New Year's Eve we enjoyed the annual town square party which that year turned out to be one of the biggest in the country with over 100,000 packing the cobbles to watch the musical spectacle. The numerical countdown from ten to one finished with fireworks whooshing high into the night as a multitude of eyes peered into the inky black sky. I was again next to Marta and was again that wondering infant, and as 2006 disappeared and 2007 introduced itself, I held her close and as tight as could be.

CHAPTER THIRTEEN

FINIS PRINCIPIO

Thursday 29th October 2015.

As I write I am sitting alone in Fareham gazing out of a flat window onto a rain-sodden street below. The sky has a stratocumulus blanket wrapped around it. And that saucy inker E L James will be disappointed because in this murk and drizzle there is only one shade of grey. It looks like the day is crying and its tears are beating on the pane and snaking their way down to form little pools on the sills. A small spider rolls haphazardly from a web in the corner of the window like a tumble-weed in a Clint Eastwood western.

I have just re-read and edited this whole narrative, ironing out its many inconsistencies, correcting grammar or punctuation, and fleshing out its weaker areas. But to be honest there weren't that many. Not because I'm just a prolific writer blessed with the talent of a Shakespeare or a Dickens, but because what I have written is largely the truth. And truth is never convoluted is it? Truth is from the heart. It must always be so. People say 'write about what you know' and that's true, but 'write about what you feel' resonated with me to a greater extent. I have laid my whole life bare for the unseen reader and to me anything short of the truth would have been a fallacy. I have chosen to reveal myself in this way for the love I have experienced with Marta. A story that needed to be told. And there is more, much more. But to tell more I should bring the present script to its natural conclusion. The lounge-room clock is ticking. The fridge is humming in the corner of the kitchen. Outside the day remains as quiet and as still as if all of life is holding its breath and waiting for me to conclude my great work.

To this end I kick off my slippers and put my coffee cup down on the side table and at once I am back Among The Poles.

January and February 2007.

Something was happening to me at this time. I had reached a turning point in my life. A new direction was taking me on a journey without a visible destination or ending. I was trundling onwards oblivious to anything. Marta became my new outlet in life. She began to seem ever more important and I felt like a different person because of this. Love had no barriers; neither language nor culture could divide us. By this time I felt more able to communicate in Polish wherever I went. At least basically, and with Marta as back-up I was practically fluent! Work-wise I found that the more I threw myself into my job at the English School the more fun I got out of it. I was made editor of the school newsletter around this time and started to take on more lessons and work extra hours. Students would look upon me for guidance in a way that I thought commanded a little bit of respect. At least. The Head of Department whose name was Lee proclaimed me to be one of the star teachers of that year's crop of tutorial reprobates. As well as my Rock Club I was also put in charge of the Monthly Literary Club. Once a month we would all meet, students and teachers, in a local pub or bar and talk about what we had been studying in class of late. A sort of discussion club if you like. I was tasked with the planning and the entertaining – which sounds quite a responsible position but in reality just meant wopping out a few A4 posters advertising the event and then subsequently turning up to the event. Those blasted clubs never really stuck to the point. They always started off with good intentions but within a few seconds or so would lapse swiftly into stupid contests involving loudness, iniquity, and drinking vodka through straws!

Said I, "So let's start today's discussion. London in the 18th and 19th centuries. In the mid to late 1800s London's East End was a byword for squalor. With regard to the temperance movement, social cleansing and Dr Barnardo, how do you think things began to change?" Students looked on with a mixture of expectation and confusion. I continued.

"Do you know, Portsmouth, near to where I live in Fareham is actually the birthplace of Charles Dickens?

Do you think collectively that Dylan Thomas22 was a better poet with or without a belly full of alcohol?

Can we perhaps liken him to your own Adam Mickiewicz?23 And if so, how?

In order to achieve any kind of brilliance must we in fact suffer first?

Do you know, Southampton, near to where I live in Fareham is actually the place where the ill-fated Titanic set sail from in 1912?"

Students looked sporadically fascinated to a point, until presently one would pipe up, "To co, pijemy coś czy nie?"

Which simple yet direct phrase would halt my London discourse before it really got going and see the table in front of us all fill up quickly and heave under several bottles of Absolut or Luksusowa. With a box of straws probably and a few bowls of salty snacks to ensure thirst was never too far away.

Poland was where I first tried my hand at karaoke. My Britney Spears is still an eye-opener and my quaint version of the Bee Gees 'How Deep is your Love' might just outlive me! For anyone who has seen this I whole-heartedly apologise. It is probably a 'no' from Simon Cowell, though he himself is of the same ilk as the Brothers Gibb – all tight trousers and all. At least give me a point for trouser-based attention to detail Cowell!

For anyone who hasn't yet seen it I can refer them and the rest of the honourable reading public to YouTube. It will come. I don't yet tweet for I am a bit of an addict when it comes to Facebook and that is enough for me at the moment. Plus I know that too many tweets do invariably make a twat.

Occasionally at these club meetings we would read out short stories or extracts we had written – either by the students or the teachers sometimes. Feedback and comment would then ensue of course. Mostly these were average run-of-the-mill type ramblings of over-active imaginations eager for some form of literary recognition. Some were in broken English and made translation difficult and often resulted in no real sense or meaning. But sometimes one student or teacher would come up with something that commanded some attention. Sometimes. And then all at once the vodka would cease its naughtiness. I recall one such time quite clearly and which illustrates the above point nicely.

We had all sat down at some table or other in a quiet corner of a coffee bar which did actually sell alcohol too, so it was both debonair and risqué. A young teacher called John subsequently asked us all if we wanted to hear his latest effort. A short story. He was in his early twenties I suppose, and a bit of a live-wire. His tale was OK – but he had us all on edge, umpteen pairs of eyes all fixed on him till he reached the end of his piece – the coffee bar reeking not of beans but of shock as he began recounting his story. What generated the fear, collectively, was his insistence that what we were about to hear was in fact a true story and something which had happened to him a few weeks previous. It started thusly:

THE PERFECT MURDER

A SHORT STORY

It had been remarkably and rather surprisingly easy. Up until that point I had not really known definitively whether I was capable of taking such a life. But take one I did, and triumphantly at that. Afterwards, overcome with elation, I took myself off to bed.

That night all those years ago still gets to me. Turning my stomach with pangs with what now has become out and out guilt. Why wasn't there another way? Perhaps there was but I was too selfish or stubborn to see it clearly at the time. Then there was the fear. Fear of committing the deed. And fear of failure.

As I recall that horrific night, and the chain of events that led to me doing what I ultimately did, I am wracked with emotion.

Yet that from the beginning, I was steeled though to do what I did, there can be no doubt.

The evening itself had started much like any other. I had returned from work – a busy day tutoring no less, eaten a rather hefty meal and had settled down in front of the television. After what seemed like hours but now I realise was probably more like minutes, I slumped lazily into the sofa. The heat outside almost sultry. The sun still shining and beating down upon the earth below. A parched earth below. The evening seemed to stand still, time likewise, almost moving in slow motion, to make way for what was to come. It was as though all of humanity was waiting for something to happen.

My eyelids heavy, a dusty haze enveloped the open balcony, and all at once I drifted off to sleep. Sometime later I was nudged awake. Something was there in the room. With me. Something unwanted, something alien. In my delirium I failed to take in the severity or the presumed danger I was in.

Another brush or nudge, a sound, then another. Finding consciousness fast I moved across the room and gathered some bearings. I was not alone.

I saw it almost immediately. A figure, a shape, dark yet not black, it moved with demonic ease from corner to corner, through the shadows of the room thrown by the now setting sun and the huge buckled arms of the giant oaks beyond the balcony.

Whether or not I was in mortal danger I knew not, for it never directly threatened my being, moving as it was deftly and confidently as though I was the intruder in my own domain. Yet it exuded dread. I knew that. Had it seen me? Does it know I'm here? Questions bred a hatred somewhere deep inside of me. I would not have this! This was my space, this ripped sofa, this torn wallpaper, this faded turkey rug.

There was nothing here to take, nothing of real value anyway. Nothing that anybody could want. Then like a bolt of realisation I sensed something.

A voice – an inner understanding. A knowledge of what would happen next. He would realise himself in time that here there was nothing to take and his menace would react thusly. He would take my life! I thought I could see this, however unrealistic it sounds to me now, recounting these awful events of many years ago. I reasoned in this way, and that gut feeling, that sense of foreboding or portent was, and still is my defence.

He did not of course take my life, for I, in an instant had made my fateful decision. I would take his!

Now resolved to this end I watched, both of us instilled in shadow.

The distance between us not more than five metres. Now I became the hunter, he the hunted. The tables reversed. Still moving, rustling papers atop the writing desk in one corner of the room, I saw my chance. He paused and I edged forward. For the first time I saw what I took to be bars or stripes of golden yellow adorning his black attire. A cloak or cape. An intricate design. Perhaps an animal of means? But here was a thing. He was sized differently. Dressed differently. And he moved in a wholly different manner altogether. And then the sound. He never spoke throughout our confrontation yet somehow seemed to communicate his intentions through me. A dull guttural tone. His whole being spoke. Words, voices, sounds coming from within him almost. I stood opposite him, behind the room's central divide, hidden yet exposed.

One more step and you will see me, feel me, hear me. My intentions cementing themselves still further. I saw where he'd been. The curtain twitched a flash of yellow, that low hellish moan or hum of... What? What did he feel? Frustration, anger, and in that an intent to meter out his revenge?

I saw my time had come. It was now or never. There could be no going back. A lumbering weapon in my hand I brazenly yet silently moved into view. Now breathing the same air, yet still he did not see me!

I called out to him. Nothing. I called out again. This time he turned and in a sudden quick movement I raised my weapon and sunk it deep into his dark body of exposed colour!

He fell in a heap to his knees, enraptured perhaps, as if he was begging for something. Food, money, life, it was too late.

As I looked on he slipped down silently onto the turkey rug he was so gallantly parading upon only seconds before.

He was dead for sure.

I can't really recall what I did immediately after this. What happened? The recollection has faded. I know I felt that sense of elation I mentioned before – but for what? Who had won? Him or me?

I am reminded, punished every day for the deed I committed. A folly of life. My sullied heart of deceit.

No-one knows. It is a deception of sorts. I have deceived all who may have had an interest in him. My dark intruder. For I know he did not sail alone and this irks me so.

The following morning I awoke early having slept peacefully and with no apparent afterthought over what I had done in the hours previous. I went to work and then went shopping. I think I even played billiards with a few close friends, all unsuspecting as they were, and as they have always been.

I don't live in that house anymore with its dark corners, shadowy divides and eerie trees overhanging the balcony. Something shielded me there from all fear of reprisals and of discovery. Yet its secret consumes me daily.

I did kill him perfectly, but within that perfection I think I also killed a part of myself.

For I don't think I could do the same thing a second time. The mess, the twisted body, the carpet, the noise. I have been rendered squeamish and European hornets are much bigger than wasps or flies.

He looked up at the rest of us peering at him in abject horror and laughed.

"Fooking A," came one cry from a young teacher from Newcastle already slightly drunk. We had to admit too that it was.

As we stood our shot glasses up and refilled them in relief, John carried on talking. It turned out he'd been writing for some months himself after meeting a Korean teacher in Warsaw who was working for the 'Voice' newspaper. 'The Warsaw Voice' was a periodical I knew well. It is an English language newspaper and is read in part though not exclusively, by the English. John's friend was called Min. I asked John whether he still saw this Min being as I was not a little bit intrigued.

"We're still in touch mate. He's a bit busy obviously but I could probably get his number if you want?"

I did want.

He went on in the same vein, "The last time I saw him he was working on a piece about revenge or something, for a magazine or whatever. I think he's got a website. It might be on there."

At the risk of sounding like Szesherezade24 staving off her death by telling King Shariah bawdy tales of intrigue and such like, this is what he told me:

"We were at Min's place a few weeks ago, you know talking about stuff. He said he liked 'A Christmas Carol' by Dickens and we got talking about that being as it was early December. He passed me a small red copy of the masterpiece in question which I had never seen before. It was about five inches by three, printed in 1977 by Book Club Associates. I was partial to Dickens too and on taking the small book from him quoted the line, "Marley was dead, to begin with," the first sentence from the story. Min laughed and looked surprised and we talked more on what was a shared liking of good old Charles. After a few drinks and a bite to eat we went out to meet a few of his friends at a local pizza bar. Once ensconced inside and with his mates pouring over the menu wondering if a Margherita or a Hot and Spicy would be the way to go, Min showed me a story he had been working on and asked if I would like to hear it."

"Of course" I said.

"And so off he went, reading from a bundle of notes he had in front of him. I listened to his queer little tale of misplaced trust and revenge as I supped my drink. His tale is etched into my mind more or less and if I remember well enough went something like this..."

REVENGE IS SWEET

A SHORT STORY

Alan hadn't long been married. A matter of months had passed only since the knot had been well and truly tied.

Alan, the chancer. The ladies' man. The loveable rogue. Everyone had an opinion on him and it was usually one of the above. Did he have a feeling heart though? His friends and close family thought so, while everyone else, business colleagues, acquaintances and so on, perhaps deeply entrenched on the other side of the fence. One thing most could agree on though was that he really did like the ladies a bit too much and always had.

Ellie had hoped she could change all this. A straight girl with a good upbringing, her father a priest no less, she loved Alan and wanted so much for that love to be worth something. Ellie was younger, five years nearly, having just turned thirty.

Her family had insisted she marry the day before her birthday in fact, her father instigating the majority of the occasion, while her mother smiled meekly at her somewhat overbearing husband.

"Oh Richard, Ellie is old enough to make her own decisions. She's thirty for Christ's sake, sorry for Pete's sake, let her loose a bit."

Richard frowned. "I'm only saying if there's to be a wedding and if there's to be a birthday for the girl, why not combine the two? It makes sense Babs. Financial sense if nothing else."

Ellie went with her father on this one, as she often did. Part of her agreed about the money idea, but a greater part of her reasoned that a wedding and a birthday on the same weekend might appeal to Alan's sense of romance, thus tightening the bond between them from the off.

Alan was indeed romantic, that cannot be denied. But was his romance now strictly reserved for Ellie alone? She lay awake at night worrying over this but would eventually fall asleep amid dreams of princes in shining white armour riding proudly through untouched gardens of Edens.

Alan turned on his computer at home. Social media had been shouting about the wedding day now for months with friends and relatives all posting, poking and liking or whatever it is people do to express empathy or emotion these days.

Ellie was at her parent's house when she received an email.

"Hi. On my own. A bit bored. Gonna make myself a spot of lunch then sort out the jobs you left darling. Hope Rich and Babs are OK. Be up at the weekend. See you at 6pm. I'll meet you halfway as usual. Love A."

Halfway was the pub the couple often met up in after work in the evenings. Tonight Alan had booked a table for two. There was to be champagne to compliment a lovely meal.

Ellie smiled and sent a quick reply.

"Can't wait A. All fine here. Dad's just going through some stuff with me. I'll have the steak and gammon tonight. See you at 6. E."

Alan looked up from the screen and closed it gently. He glanced across the room at Nikki who was preparing a light lunch, and who was softly singing to herself.

"You want ketchup or mayo darling?" she called out.

"Actually is there any hot sauce in the cupboard?"

Nikki opened the door and peered inside.

"Plenty" before turning back to Alan, "but you don't want to overdose, you'll be getting all the hot sauce you can possibly desire after lunch." Nikki adopted that sultry Latino look that she knew drove Alan wild as she looked deeply into his eyes.

A flash of suspender and lunch was perhaps understandably forgotten, as the couple lurched with what resembled drunken abandon towards the bedroom.

Ellie and her father, her mother being out, were discussing the wedding and pouring over the photos.

"You remember Uncle Dave? What did he wear to the reception, father?"

Richard thought for a minute and with a sudden grasp of realisation nodded.

"Yes," he exhaled, a knowing hum of a sound, "Hardly appropriate was it? But that's Uncle Dave I suppose. If he felt turning up to a wedding reception looking like Noddy, is it, then who are we to argue. It's just his way my dear."

Ellie looked thoughtfully at her father, "That's it, you know. Funnily enough some mates also said the same thing. I mean that he reminded them of Noddy."

Ellie seemed to wear a pained expression as she looked up at her father and said "And his blessed daughter, almost as if she wore his clothes. A female Noddy."

The two of them put down the album, drained their coffees and walked through to the hallway laughing quietly to themselves.

"Come on" said Richard, "it's time."

Alan, having arrived a quarter of an hour early, sat down at the table in the small pub that was halfway. Thinking of Nikki and of what had just passed he felt no pangs of guilt. He looked up and beckoned the waitress.

"Single Bells, no ice" he glanced up at the pretty girl dressed in a black pinafore and white blouse.

"And one for yourself, love, if you want."

The waitress thanked him but declined.

"Company policy I'm afraid" she explained.

"Your loss" thought Alan, as he picked up his phone. A short message to Nikki was followed by one to Ellie.

"Hi sweetheart. I'm at the pub. Got here a bit early to get table. See you in 10."

Alan put his phone down on the table and reached into his left trouser pocket. He picked out a short note from Nikki. Glancing down at it he read it out in surprise.

"Thanks for today stud. Same time next week I'm guessing? You know there's a crack in your ceiling don't you Mr?"

Alan grinned and screwed up the piece of paper before taking himself off to the toilets where he ripped it into several dozen snippets and finally placed it into a standing waste basket.

He re-entered the pub and sat back down at his table.

Nikki had been a fixture for a number of months now. He'd actually met her at the wedding. She was one of the relatives on Richard's side. He'd picked her out then. A happy-go-lucky sort of girl. Confident there was no doubt. Eccentric too. She'd fascinated Alan to the point where they'd spent nearly half an hour chatting in one corner of the hotel venue.

"Poor Ellie" folk commented.

"He should be entertaining all his guests as host and groom shouldn't he?"

"Yeah, not flirting with that little strumpet eh?" came several other retorts.

Ellie thought little of it at the time and the couple were soon doing the newly-wed thing with etiquette. But a wandering eye does nowt but wander.

As Alan mused and reflected on this with not an ounce or a shred of guilt etched upon his face, the door opened. He got up and pushed out a chair for his wife.

"Bang on time I see Els. What are we drinking?"

Almost before she could reply the door behind them opened for a second time and in walked an older man.

Alan looked up in surprise.

"Richard! What are you doing here?"

Father and daughter said not a word but handed Alan an envelope before strangely and calmly walking off into the night. They did not look back.

With confusion Alan tore open the envelope. A small piece of paper fell onto his lap, followed by a short document made up of several sheets of paper.

Upon the piece of paper and written in Ellie's handwriting were the words:

"*Noddy doesn't live in Toytown."*

The documents were of course divorce papers.

"Well, what do you think then?" Min said upon reading the last line. "A dish best served cold?"

I don't think any of us actually did comment on it to be honest. We just nodded and bowed to his genius - real or otherwise, and tucked into the pizza.

John laughed as he remembered the occasion. "You know – I'll chuck you his contact details if you're interested?"

I thanked him and drained my glass.

The rest of the evening went by in a cloud of vapour and befuddlement and culminated as a lot of Polish parties often did and still do, way past midnight.

I slunk wearily home and edged myself drunkenly into bed next to Marta about 4am. As was often the case after a big night out where Polish beer or vodka had been involved I quickly dropped off to sleep which was probably more like a coma. World War Three would not have woken me that night. Had Blair given the 45 minute warning I still would have had no chance. No chance of adopting the correct set of punitively important procedures, Raymond Briggs25 showed us in 'When the Wind Blows.'

No matter – for in the coming days and weeks I was to deliver my own 'weapon of mass destruction' that would change my life, Marta's life, and the lives of all those around us ten-fold. And I didn't have to sex anything up or write any dossiers of a dodgy kind. Chilcot could inquire all he liked.

Towards the middle of February I found myself in the centre of town drinking in a little sports bar called 'The Warka Bar.' It was a nice-looking bar full of pictures of famous sportsmen and women, and with about half a dozen big screens scattered around the place lest you missed a piece of the action whilst coming out of the toilets or whatever. I remember I was watching an English championship football match, whether Leeds or Charlton though I now fail to recall but it was on and I was passing the time. Marta was at her parent's house in Góra and was to meet me that same day.

I was reflecting in that pub. Reflecting on my life and what now lay ahead for me. Earlier that day I had met up with the Jewish girl Jamie who was ecstatic as her boyfriend, Scott, had just arrived from the US. The smile on her face widening as she told me. I smiled too as I recollected the American scamp staring at me as I took a tiddle in his girlfriend's flat a few months back. This guy's name was Scott. He was a good-looking chap of good family stock. Or so I imagined. His hair was long and frizzy, like he'd had a perm back in the 80s and it had refused to go away. He wore glasses that made him look clever and studious, but also slightly clownish. He was a great fellow. Jamie now had her soulmate and someone she could travel and explore with. And someone she could take to Jewish restaurants and be comfortable that everything would be understood.

It was around this time that Melissa visited us and we introduced her to all the Polish comrades. She was a big hit with the guys at school. I went to meet her off the plane at Wrocław's old airport terminal which has now closed. A bigger, more modern terminal opened up a few years ago a little further out of town and is now fully operational. The old one was much smaller but still had everything you could possibly require in an airport. Round the back of the terminal itself there was a fence where you could watch the planes taking off and coming in to land. I knew Mel's plane was due to land so went outside and peered through the fence and watched. In the blue morning sky I saw her plane lugging its way towards me. Still a distance away. The black shape slowly increasing in size and descending all the while. As it landed it taxied away from the terminal and returned some minutes later. The doors opened and the steps were brought up to aid the passengers down onto Polish hallowed soil. The weather I should add here was particularly cold. It had been snowing for a few days on and off. I waited and observed as all the passengers started to file slowly towards arrivals.

"Where was she?" I questioned.

Then I caught sight of her. Dressed in a purple top and long black dress and carrying a small dark handbag she began her own descent. I smiled with excitement. Then all of sudden that smile wiped itself from my face as Mel, in her eagerness I suspect to get into Poland, tripped on the icy steps and her dress, (though possibly not in that order) and fell into the country for the first time! She must've fallen from about halfway off those airport passenger steps. At the bottom, sprawled out on the runway like some twopenny wench-lady, I watched in horror as a security guard hoisted her up and helped her on her way. She was not hurt too much, though her pride was battered and she sported a large gash on her left knee that wouldn't stop bleeding for a good few hours. Melissa told me all this as we sat in the airport lounge sipping a Polish beer and catching up on all the gossip. I didn't want to embarrass her further by telling her that I had in fact witnessed the whole thing from afar, from the fence. So I didn't. Some things are better left unsaid. I do hope she doesn't get her hands on this work!

She stayed in Poland for about a week and we had a lot of fun. It was this, among other things, I was reflecting on in that Warka bar.

Some things you know will instantly change your life. My decision to come to Poland did change my life. But it was only one of many life-changing adventures that buzzed around me in that country and at that time. And so I began a kind of restoration I suppose. It was indeed like being completely reborn.

Two weeks previous to my Warka Bar reverie we had ventured out for a family meal at a nearby restaurant. Myself, Marta and her parents. Over a lovely table of hunters stew and vegetables and based on the last two and a half years of my rebirth, I suddenly and deliberately became awfully officious.

I announced that on September 15th 2007 we would be married.

EXPLANATORY NOTES

By Gary Alan Motley

There follows an excerpt explaining some of the more abstract or oblique references mentioned in the text. I have attempted to define and make clear most of the literary points that have been raised particularly where they refer to authors or poets from earlier centuries. I have also listed some of the bibliographic sources from whence those references were taken.

All names and source material correspond to the numbered footnotes within the text and have been listed here in chapter order and in the order in which they appear within that chapter.

1. C S LEWIS – (Clive Staples Lewis) - Early twentieth century author poet essayist and critic best known for works including The Screwtape Letters and The Space Trilogy and of the volumes known collectively as The Chronicles of Narnia focusing on a magical world of that same name. Captivating children and adults alike, Lewis's books have not aged. When read, from publication right up to the present day, thraldom continues to follow. Lewis was born in 1898 and died in 1963. He did not according to my knowledge ever visit Bexleyheath.

2. BROTHERS GRIMM – (Jacob 1785-1863 and Wilhelm 1786-1859) - Nineteenth century authors of numerous moral tales of woe and intrigue ostensibly aimed at children but enjoyed just as much by adults. Jacob and Wilhelm knew great poverty growing up and on attending the University of Marburg they developed a taste for German folklore. With their frequent use and depiction of small innocent young children in flowery dresses lost in forests or abandoned by their parents the Grimm brothers would almost certainly be investigated by Yewtree today.

3. E L JAMES – (Erika Mitchell) - Writer of the recent bawdy sadomasochistic Fifty Shades trilogy. James was born in 1963 and was schooled in Buckinghamshire before further study at the University of Kent. James began writing the Fifty Shades books in 2009 which were loosely inspired by the

vampire novel series Twilight. The works include descriptions of graphic sex and bondage. A self-made millionaire James is married with two sons and is oblivious to the countless people masturbating to her saucy narratives.

4. L FRANK BAUM – (Lyman Frank Baum) – Born in 1856 in New York Baum wrote mainly children's books and is perhaps best known for his depiction of the fantasy series The Wonderful Wizard of Oz. The author penned numerous sequels and various other fantasy novels. He married in 1882 and had four sons. Baum died in Los Angeles in 1919. Insinuations that his end was brought on by the awful realisation that he held an embarrassing name were proved to be unfounded.

5. WILLIAM SHAKESPEARE – Shakespeare wrote the comedy AS YOU LIKE IT in or around 1599 and saw the work published in The First Folio in 1623. The piece has many characters including the two noted in 'Among the Poles.' A court jester or local fool called Touchstone who lusts after a young country girl by the name of Audrey. The play includes one of Shakespeare's most famous speeches 'All the World's a Stage' and takes place largely in a place called 'The Forest of Arden' where dogging is said to have originated from.

6. MARCEL PROUST – French novelist essayist and critic Proust was born in 1871 and died in 1922. His work 'A la recherché do temps perdu' or in English 'In Search of Lost Time' was overwhelmingly his most well- known project. A vast undertaking it remains to date one of the longest novels ever written consisting of over 9 million characters spread over seven volumes. It was published in seven parts between 1913 and 1927 and contained themes such as memory, homosexuality, separation, anxiety and the nature of art. Proust as a boy was a sickly child and suffered both with asthma and constipation. He was said in part neurotic and a nostalgist and to be a 'mother's child' and indeed did enjoy a close relationship with his mother Jeanne Clemence Weil. Educationally the young Proust excelled in literature and among his classmates he gathered many anecdotes and stories that were later to form a part of his novel and many of which centred around the bourgeoisie. Proust signed up to join the French Army in the late 1880s and continued working on his great work. In 1922-1931 C.K Scott Moncrieff was among the first to translate the piece into English and the title thus became 'Remembrance of Things Past.' The novel includes a notable section which varies in length from 17 to 30 pages, depending on the version, recounting how the author turns over in bed and which is referred to in 'Among The Poles.' Sometimes said to be homosexual, a claim that he denied, Proust's language was without question floral and his colourful description of asparagus (in the first volume 'Swann's Way') and a chamber pot for me only says one thing. Gay.

7. MAREK KRAJEWSKI – A Polish writer and linguist Krajewski was born in Wrocław, formally the German city of Breslau in 1966. Best known for his Chandleresque novels with detective Eberhard Mock as the protagonist. Set in pre-war Wrocław the works are dark and atmospheric and feature mutilation and other forms of death as a subject matter proving once again that everyone loves a murder. Particularly if you have committed one.

8. M R JAMES - (Montague Rhodes James) – Author scholar and provost of both King's College Cambridge and of Eton College James was born in 1862. His work as a medievalist is regarded well enough though his collection of ghost stories is perhaps best known. Among his various tales of ghosts and ghostly goings-on is one called THE MEZZOTINT published in 1904 and which centres on an old picture which changes in appearance over the course of some days. The picture shows an idyllic garden with a house at the end to begin with. Later the same picture shows the same scene but with a man and his shadow seen creeping towards the house in the foreground. Subsequent scenes show the shadowy figure lurking ever closer towards the big house and ending with him stealing away with a small child dead or otherwise in his arms. Ghost stories of this ilk are said not to be as popular today due to the advance in technology science and the decline in use of laudanum.

9. DANTE'S CIRCLES OF HELL – (DANTE ALIGHIERI) - Inferno the first part of Dante's DIVINE COMEDY follows the Roman poet Virgil who accompanies Dante into the underworld or The 9 Circles of Hell from Limbo to Treachery. Dante was born around 1265 in Florence, Italy. He was a statesman, poet, and language and political theorist. His literary and theoretical descriptions of Heaven Purgatory and Hell have given inspiration with regard to Western art and are said to have influenced many works of Shakespeare, Chaucer and Milton among others. Despite extensive readings no mention of Anne Robinson or Harriet Harman have been discovered anywhere near The 9 Circles.

10. JOHN CLELAND – Baptised in 1709 Cleland was an English novelist best known for his MEMOIRS OF A WOMAN OF PLEASURE or FANNY HILL a highly pornographic and sexual novel for the time. Cleland's use of such eroticised material (Fanny Hill herself being 15) including homosexual fornication caused offence and led to censorship of the work in question. Cleland attended Westminster School in 1721 and later entered the British East India Company. After being arrested and imprisoned for a debt in 1748 Cleland began writing Fanny Hill. Around 1750 the book was withdrawn and was not again published for over 100 years. Cleland died in 1789 leaving future generations of readers to enjoy his literary Fanny.

11. AHASUERUS THE WANDERING JEW – A legend focusing on the carrying of the cross by Christ to Golgoltha. The legend holds that Christ had stopped for a rest outside the house of Ahasuerus. When Ahasuerus, a shoemaker, saw the Lord he jeered Him and questioned His motives in stopping whereupon the Saviour put upon the Jew a terrible curse. The Wandering Jew Ahasuerus was made to wander the Earth without stopping until Christ returned. The story has many variations and has been adapted numerous times over the centuries. The Wandering Jew is sometimes said to a young man yet at other times distinctly old. One dramatic adaptation of the tale is the 1833 French work by Edgar Quinet, AHASVERUS. Logic might have it that Jamie and Scott in 'Among the Poles' were playing out these biblical roles. Jamie being Ahasuerus and Scott of course, Christ.

12. A A MILNE – (Alan Alexander Milne) Born in 1882 Milne wrote the Winnie the Pooh stories along with other poems. Milne was educated at his father's private school where one of the teachers was H G Wells who published WAR OF THE WORLDS in 1898. He graduated later from Trinity College, Cambridge in 1903 with a BA in mathematics. Milne was married and had one son called Christopher Robin who he cast as the little boy in the Pooh stories. He died in Hartfield, Sussex in 1956. Many scholars have since questioned his use of ambiguity particularly modernists who have declared that a better title would today be Winnie the Shit.

13. JOHNATHAN SWIFT – A satirist, essayist poet and cleric Swift was born in 1667 in Dublin. Swift is best remembered arguably for his work GULLIVER'S TRAVELS. The work was satirical and ironic and deeply political. His two styles of satire are known today as Horatian and Juvenalian. Published in 1726 the work has never been out of print. The piece is divided into four parts and charts the protagonist Gulliver as he travels to four different lands whereupon he has many adventures and meets many weird and fantastic characters. From the land called Lilliput where Gulliver is a giant and everyone else tiny, to the opposite land Brobdingnag where Gulliver is a tiny man among giants the novel is hugely satirical and makes religious allusions along with comments on the state of the European government. Swift died in 1745 also in Dublin just over two hundred years before Private Eye was published and where he would almost certainly have been employed today.

14. PHILIP LARKIN - Born in 1922 in Warwickshire Larkin was a poet novelist and librarian. He graduated from Oxford in 1943 and subsequently went on to work in the library at the University of Hull where he kept his post for thirty years. Rumoured to be a traditional man who disliked public life and shunned fame in itself, Larkin also had a liking for pornography, in particular top-shelf literature. Larkin also turned down the position of Poet Laureate in 1984 after the death of Sir John Betjeman. After contracting cancer of the oesophagus Larkin died in 1985 aged just 63 too early for any hard drive of his to have been seized and scrutinised.

15. HORACE - (ARS POETICA) - Written by Horace in 19 BC ARS POETICA or The 'Art of Poetry' is the author's attempt to advise poets on how best to write good poetry. Containing around 476 lines and many maxims to boot and scribed in hexameter verse the work was first translated into English by Thomas Drant in 1566 and later by Ben Jonson in 1640. It is a piece that has influenced many poets since and with its countless poetic phrases and quotations has long since become a work of immense merit and substance. Not having seen the original of course I'm suspicious that 'Printed in 19 BC' may have been inscribed on the first page rendering the whole a complete farce.

16. THOMAS HARDY - A Victorian novelist and poet Hardy wrote in both genres though considered himself more of a poet. Influenced by Wordsworth and Dickens Hardy was born in 1840. His many literary works now world classics include 'Far from the Madding Crowd' 'Tess of the d'Urbervilles' and 'Jude the Obscure' and focused on social upheavals and suffering. A realist at heart Hardy really got into the passions of his protagonists and aligned them with class divisions and inferiority particularly of women. In 'Tess of the d'Urbervilles' Hardy wrote "...as peculiar, probably, to the rural labourer as the hexagon to the bee" noting the bee's strange preference for the hexagon as opposed to more simplified shapes in building their honeycombs. A believer in social reform Hardy's work was admired by many younger authors including D H Lawrence and Virginia Woolf. Married twice Hardy died in 1928 aged 87 and since he was married twice and he didn't write it, his death did not occur in a Bleak House.

17. MR FEZZIWIG'S BALL (CHARLES DICKENS) - This occasion or event happens in 'A CHRISTMAS CAROL' (1843) by Charles Dickens. It represents a party held by Mr Fezziwig - a character created by Dickens to contrast with Ebenezer Scrooge and his attitudes to money and business ethics. Fezziwig is portrayed as a jovial and happy-go-lucky business man and throws a lavish Christmas party for all his workers together with his friends and family. Fezziwig as a fictional character was played by Brian Bedford in the 2004 film 'A Christmas Carol' (The Musical) which also starred Kelsey Grammer as Ebenezer Scrooge. The Fezziwig Ball in the story was unlike that of Hitler in that the character had many - indeed threw them annually.

18. ALDOUS HUXLEY - (BRAVE NEW WORLD) - A novel published in 1932 and set in 2540 BRAVE NEW WORLD is a story which attempts to predict how society as a whole might change over time. With heavy emphasis on science and developments in technology and psychology particularly methods to condition the brain Huxley's novel is a dystopian masterpiece. In 2000 British heavy metal group Iron Maiden released an album entitled Brave New World which depicted a

futuristic London on its cover. The novel itself might be a dystopian read but the song should you listen to Maiden will leave you needing to plaster up your bleeding ears. And should Iron Maiden still be around in 2540 there will be a song about bleeding ears too I suspect.

19. THE CHARGE OF THE LIGHT BRIGADE - A poem written in 1854 by ALFRED LORD TENNYSON. The poem recounts the bravery of the Light Brigade at the Battle of Balaclava during the Crimean War. Led by Lord Cardigan six hundred men were honoured after charging the Russian cavalry and Cossacks costing over 100 lives. Tennyson was said to have written the poem after reading an account of the atrocities in The Times newspaper. The assault was the result of miscommunication at the time but later enhanced the reputation of the British cavalry. Coincidently British heavy metal group Iron Maiden recorded a song called 'The Trooper' in 1983 about the very same incident. Complete with black and white 'footage' of the event it proves once again that Maiden have been at the forefront of British history and folklore. And were in all probability even there.

20. RIME OF THE ANCIENT MARINER - Written in 1797 by SAMUEL TAYLOR COLERIDGE The Rime of the Ancient Mariner is the longest and perhaps most famous of Coleridge's poems. Regarded as an epic the work was first published in the poet's Lyrical Ballads in 1798. Coleridge was at the forefront of British Romanticism and in creating his masterpiece here has influenced many that have come after him. In short the poem tells the tale of a merchant seaman who shoots an albatross at sea and thereafter has to suffer the consequences. The dead bird is hung around his neck and his crew all perish as a deathly curse takes hold of the ship. As the poem continues the Ancient Mariner is spared though at a cost. He must wander the Earth retelling his tale to all that pass him by. The moral being that Man must love all things that God created. The reference within 'Among the Poles' relates to a passage in the poem concerning the abundance of water and the existence of a 'painted ship upon a painted ocean.' Coleridge was born in 1772 and died in 1834. He was married to Sarah Fricker. The couple had four children. A frequent user of opiates I have no doubt that the poet used Huxley's image of the future and conjured up a surreal picture of Bob Geldof to complete his work and so that one day an obscure author might stumble upon the connection himself. (Incidentally, with regard to Iron Maiden, in 1984....)

21. SENSE AND SENSIBLIITY - (JANE AUSTEN) - Published in 1811 under the name 'A Lady' Sense and Sensibility was a work of romantic fiction. It is set in south-west England as well as London and Kent and tells the story of the Dashford sisters and in particular Marianne and Elinor. Often billed as a 'comedy of manners' as a genre the novel satirises social class and division. Austen characterises Marianne as an attractive woman deeply romantic and intelligent and frank. In contrast Elinor is sensible and responsible and seems to care more for others than herself. She is sometimes thus seen as cold and aloof. Austen was born in 1775 and is perhaps regarded most highly for her second novel 'Pride and Prejudice' published two years after Sense and Sensibility. Writing as someone who has several alter-egos I can categorically say that I can sympathise with both Marianne and Elinor and their respective personalities. I can also say that perversely I fancy them both.

22. DYLAN THOMAS – Poet, and writer Dylan Thomas was born in Swansea, Wales in 1914. Married in 1939 to Caitlin Macnamara the couple went on to have three children. He seemed over the years to epitomise the cliché of 'The Doomed Poet' being as he was a 'friend of alcohol.' He personally remarked upon this analogy himself. Thomas produced many radio broadcasts in the 1940s one of which was 'A Child's Christmas in Wales' and was seen as a pioneer within this medium. His style often being modernism or romanticism he wrote many well-known pieces including 'Do not go gentle into that good night' and 'Under Milk Wood' based around a small fictional village which he called 'Llareggub' which he rather amusingly had to change on several occasions due to the fact that the word 'Llareggub' in reverse spelled 'Bugger All.' During the early 1950s Thomas moved to America where his drinking worsened and in 1953 at the age of 39 he died of pneumonia and brain swelling which many have attributed to his excessive use of alcohol. In connection to his liking for amusing wordplay I have in fact uncovered a rather apt example myself. Perhaps on reflection and after this we should have seen it coming. 'Under Milk Wood' is an anagram of 'Woe! I'm old drunk!'

23. ADAM MICKIEWICZ – Born in Poland in December 1798 Mickiewicz was a Polish poet, essayist, dramatist and publicist. He also became a professor of Slavic literature. In addition he was seen as a political activist and inspired various uprisings within Poland as a country. As to his literary works he is regarded as the 'national poet' in Poland, Lithuania and Belarus and has been compared to Byron with regards to his style and 'voice'. Mickiewicz is perhaps best known for works including 'Dziady' and what is considered and revered as the national epic 'Pan Tadeusz.' As a direct result of his allegiance to various groups intent on political upheaval in Poland he was jailed in 1823 and banished to Russia and lived a life effectively in exile. There are numerous monuments to him across Poland including the main square in Krakow and the śródmieście district of Warsaw. The epic Pan Tadeusz has since become the name of a popular vodka in Poland and is drunk extensively across the country along with all those who actually drink it.

24. SZESHERAZADE - 1001 NIGHTS (ARABIAN NIGHTS) - A collection of tales or stories of early middle-eastern as well as south-asian origin which have been collected and translated over hundreds of years. Dating back to at least 1300 they are, in the main, traditional folk stories often with a moral however obscure it might at first seem to be. The tales are often bawdy and include love, humour, tragedy, comedy and erotica interspersed with tradition and social etiquette. The whole centres around a frame story narrated by a young virgin called Szesherazade who is asked by King Shariah's vizier to become the king's next bride. The king has taken it upon himself to kill all his partners in revenge for his brother's cheating wife. Knowing that she is likely to be killed too Szesherazade begins telling the king the aforementioned tales of intrigue every night for 1001 nights ending each time with a cliff-hanger and leaving the king wanting more thus cleverly staving off her death until the next night whereupon she repeats the same process. There have been many copies and

translations of the tales though not all are original. 'Aladdin's Lamp' 'Ali Baba and the forty thieves' and 'The seven voyages of Sindbad' all famous and oft-told were not part of the original manuscript and have been added over the centuries. Consensus is they were added by Antoine Galland of French origin who in 1704-17 translated the first European version 'Les Milles et une nuits.' In regards to tales centring around social etiquette there is a beautiful example which brings forth both tears of laughter and sadness. To enjoy simply read 'The Historic Fart.'

25. RAYMOND BRIGGS (WHEN THE WIND BLOWS) – Briggs was born in 1934 and was a novelist, illustrator and cartoonist. His notable works include 'The Snowman' 'Father Christmas' and 'Fungus the Bogeyman.' Briggs has won many awards for his literary work including 'The Hans Christian Anderson Award' and the 'British Book Award.' In 1982 he wrote 'When the Wind Blows' a social and political slant on the events and aftermath of a nuclear attack. Inspired perhaps by the Cold War Briggs imagined what life would be like 'post-nuclear strike' from the view-point of an ordinary retired couple whom he named as Jim and Hilda Bloggs. The piece was made into a short animated film in 1986 with Sir John Mills and Dame Peggy Ashcroft voicing the characters. Briggs criticises or satirises top-level advice and naivety in the film when he gets the couple to adhere to the government's 'Protect and Survive' pamphlets. In the animation Jim Bloggs is seen comparing the impending attack to World War Two. His first wife Jean died in 1973 and Briggs now lives in Sussex with new partner Liz. What is heartening to learn is that despite such a pessimistic opus and the fact that he is now 82 and in stark contrast to most of the references alluded to here, Briggs is still alive.

AMONG THE POLES is essentially a contemporary story of love. Often frank in its literary diversions into comedic, political and sometimes controversial expression, the author as named here, Gary Alan Motley has moulded Bill Bryson, Russell Brand, Oscar Wilde and Amy Winehouse to create one bibliographic Frankenstein. Frequently amusing, sometimes high-brow and referential AMONG THE POLES charts the author's journey from romantic indifference or bleakness to committed union. The tale begins in the late 1970s where we meet the author briefly before lurching forward to the early years of the new millennium. Envisaged as a three-part work this first introduces the pivotal characters, namely the author and Marta, the love interest. It charts a growing romance between the years 2004 and 2007.

Interest is captured during the many adventures had by the author as he wades his way through his mind of emotion. From unfortunate escapades such as falling asleep on midnight trains, to surreal images of Anne Robinson and Dante's Circles of Hell, AMONG THE POLES never fails to keep the reader glued to the page. Its frequent literary or scholastic references together with its foppish language and bookish comedy are typical of a standard novella, and create a blend of light and shade, perhaps in the vein of Bill Bryson or Oscar Wilde. The brash flowery vocabulary sometimes bordering on obscenity a taste of Brand. And when sobriety is questioned we see Winehouse standing mockingly before us.

WRITTEN AND EDITED IN FAREHAM 2016

MY THANKS AND GRATITUDE IN WRITING THIS BOOK GO TO MANY AND MUST OF COURSE INCLUDE MY OWN FAMILY WHO FIGURE IN IT AS AND WHEN THEY DO. MY MOTHER BARBARA, MY SISTER CAROL, AND ESPECIALLY MY BROTHER WITHOUT WHOSE HELP I WOULD HAVE FAILED EPICALLY A LONG TIME AGO. PEOPLE WHO MOVE IN AND OUT OF THE NARRATIVE I MUST ALSO THANK. THOSE IN ENGLAND AND HOLLAND OF COURSE AND ESPECIALLY THE NUMEROUS FRIENDS FAMILY AND OTHER ACQUAINTANCES IN POLAND WHO MAY NOT EVEN HAVE READ THIS. YOU HAVE PROVIDED THE TALES I TELL AND I HAVE BEEN INSPIRED BY YOU. IN CONCLUSION, HAVING WRITTEN THE LINES ABOVE, I SAVE MY MOST HEART-FELT THANKS TO THE PEOPLE WHO ARE NOT HERE ANYMORE. PEOPLE WHO HAVE PASSED AWAY AND ARE NOT HERE TO READ THIS. I SPEAK OF COURSE OF MY GRANDPARENTS AND OF MY FATHER, GRAHAM. I HOPE SINCERELY THAT SOMEWHERE AMONG THE CLOUDS YOU CAN ENJOY THIS WORK AND KNOW THAT YOU ABOVE ALL OTHERS HAVE GIVEN ME THE INSPIRATION AND THE MOTIVATION TO ENGAGE MYSELF AND WRITE.

GARY ALAN MOTLEY

If you truly and sincerely liked reading this book then one of two things must now happen. Either you fall back into your sofa with a cup of tea and switch on the television, in your indifference. Maybe you have to pick the kids up in an hour or do the weekly grocery shopping at Asda. A swift return to normality. Alternatively you can leave a review of AMONG THE POLES so that other prospective readers, like yourself, maybe interested in flicking through its pages. Amazon will be pleased and I equally so, as through your kindly actions they, and I, will be fiscally recompensed.

Printed in Poland
by Amazon Fulfillment
Poland Sp. z o.o., Wrocław